Napoléon et son état-major à la bataille de la Moskowa, huile sur toile Vasiliy Vasilyevich Vereshagin. (Google Art Project, DR)

THE IMPERIAL GUARD OF THE FIRST EMPIRE

Part Three

1800-1815, THE MOUNTED TROOPS AND THE OTHER CORPS

Drawings by Andre JOUINEAU
Text by Jean-Marie MONGIN
Captions by Andre JOUINEAU and Jean-Marie MONGIN
Translated from the French by Alan McKAY

HEIMDAL

The Mounted Troops in the Imperial Guard

After dealing with the mounted companies and the Gendarmerie d'Elite, this third volume given over to the Imperial Guard deals with the lesser known cavalry units: The Gendarmes d'Ordonnance (the Ordnance Gendarmes), the Gardes d'Honneur (the Guards of Honour), the Lithuanian Tartars, the Krakus and the Eclaireurs (Scouts), before presenting in the last chapter the Horse Artillery, the units of the Train, and the medical service.

The gendarmerie d'elite

The Decree of 29 July 1804 (10 Thermidor Year XII) dealt with the reorganisation and transformation of the Consular Guard which became the Imperial Guard. The composition of this new unit[1] did not change. The Gendarmes' principal task was to maintain law and order in all the places where the Government, and of course the Emperor, were located. As a result, they took part in all the Empire's campaigns anywhere the General Headquarters was located.

Their duties

Apart from their ordinary duties, the Gendarmes d'Elite of the Guard provided a mounted Guard for the Tuileries Palace and the Malmaison, as well as a courier service, and the security of the Emperor's carriage, a security post on the terrace of the Tuileries Palace, on the garden side; and two security posts at the Temple Prison.

The other duties consisted of ensuring the Emperor's security and that of his entourage while travelling, escort duties and the safety of any high dignitaries and heads of foreign states visiting Imperial territory. While campaigning, the Gendarmes were incorporated into the Cavalry of the Guard. They guarded the prisoners and the trophies. All the duties and the services of the Provost at General Headquarters were taken on by the Legion. During the Russian Campaign, they were given the task of gathering in any laggards back into the army[2].

Composition

The Gendarmerie d'Elite Legion comprised two mounted two-company squadrons and a half battalion of two companies on foot, a total strength of 633 men with their headquarters. The Gendarmes d'Elite were all NCOs who came from the troop corps. The battalion on foot was disbanded on 15 April 1806.

A "second series" of Gendarmes, the Gendarmes-bis was created in 1813. They were immediately assigned to the Young Guard. The Decree of 1 March 1813 increased their strength to 1,174 men. 160 Gendarmes-cadets entered the Guard by the Decree of 16 January 1814. During the First Restoration, the Gendarmerie d'Elite Corps was disbanded on 23 April 1814. Louis XVIII created a Company of the Gendarmes des Chasses du Roi which included part of the Gendarmes d'Elite of the former Imperial Guard.

When Napoleon returned, the Gendarmerie d'Elite was reincorporated into the Guard. When the Guard was reorganised on 8 April 1815, the Gendarmes were 100-strong; their strength increased to 250, made up mainly of former Gendarmes of the Guard, of Gendarmes from the Legions inside France and the Gendarmes of the Chasses du Roi.

A detachment of the Gendarmerie took part in the Battle of Ligny and then Waterloo. On 26 September 1815, the Gendarmerie d'Elite was dismissed at Châtellerault.

The uniform

The consular order dated 21 Pluviôse An X (10 February 1802) established the uniform.

" [...] **Article 1**

The uniform of the Gendarmerie d'Elite is established as follows: national blue-coloured coat, scarlet lapels, facings and lining, blue cuffs and collar flaps; slanting pockets with scarlet piping, a blue cloth grenade on the turnbacks, silver for the officers; jacket made of chamois cloth and deerskin breeches; white buttons with a grenade in the centre with the caption Gendarmerie d'Elite. The buttons were placed out as follows: seven small ones on each lapel, three on each cuff, two on the shoulders, two big ones at the waist, three on the pockets, three above the right lapel, fifteen little ones on the jacket. White thread tress aiglets for the gendarmes, blue and silver goat's hair for the officers, with the epaulettes of their respective ranks.

National blue coat with sleeves with white and silver thread Brandenburgs for the Marechal des logis, and silver with braid on the collar for the officers. The hat was decorated with ribbon curls, silver fringes decorated in the same way, held by a big button and edged with braid which was 24 lines wide for the gendarmes, 27 lines with pinked edges for the lieutenants, thirty for the captains, thirty-four for the senior officers with a cock's plume. A l'ecuyère boots with black spurs, black boot sleeves and gaiters. Forty-line wide yellow leatherwork edged with small white thread braid for the gendarmes, and silver for the officers; the baldric plate will be white with a yellow grenade on the cartridge case and on the belt plate.

Straight cavalry sabre, yellow copper mounting for the NCOs and gendarmes and white metal for the officers, white buffalo hide sabre knot for the brigadiers and gendarmes, blue and silver goat's hair for the Marechal des logis and silver for the officers [...].

Article 2

[...] *Horse harness. Cavalry saddle according to the ordnance, cover and hoods made of national blue cloth, so-called "*à la Bourgogne*", with a white thread stripe for the gendarmes and silver for the officers, according to the model approved by the First Consul.*

Yellow bridle with studs decorated with a grenade and netting made of white braid for the NCOs and gendarmes; white studs and silver netting for the officers [...]."

The jacket was made of chamois cloth; the full-dress breeches were made of buckskin; a second pair of breeches was made of sheepskin and used for everyday dress. Both of them were yellow ochre. While marching or campaigning over-breeches fastening on the side made of unbleached cloth were worn over the skin breeches. Breeches made of blue cloth were used for

1. The Legion d'Elite was made up with brigadiers and gendarmes coming from the other 26 other Gendarmerie Legions

2. For the organisation of the Gendarmerie d'Elite after 1806, see Tome I of this same series, in the chapter about the Gendarmes à Cheval.

The Colonel-Commanding

The colonel of the Gendarmes of the Guard in 1810, after the commandant Bucquoy. *(Private Collection, RR)*

The coat of arms of Savary, Duke of Rovigo, the colonel commanding the Gendarmes of the Guard.

Major-general's epaulettes.

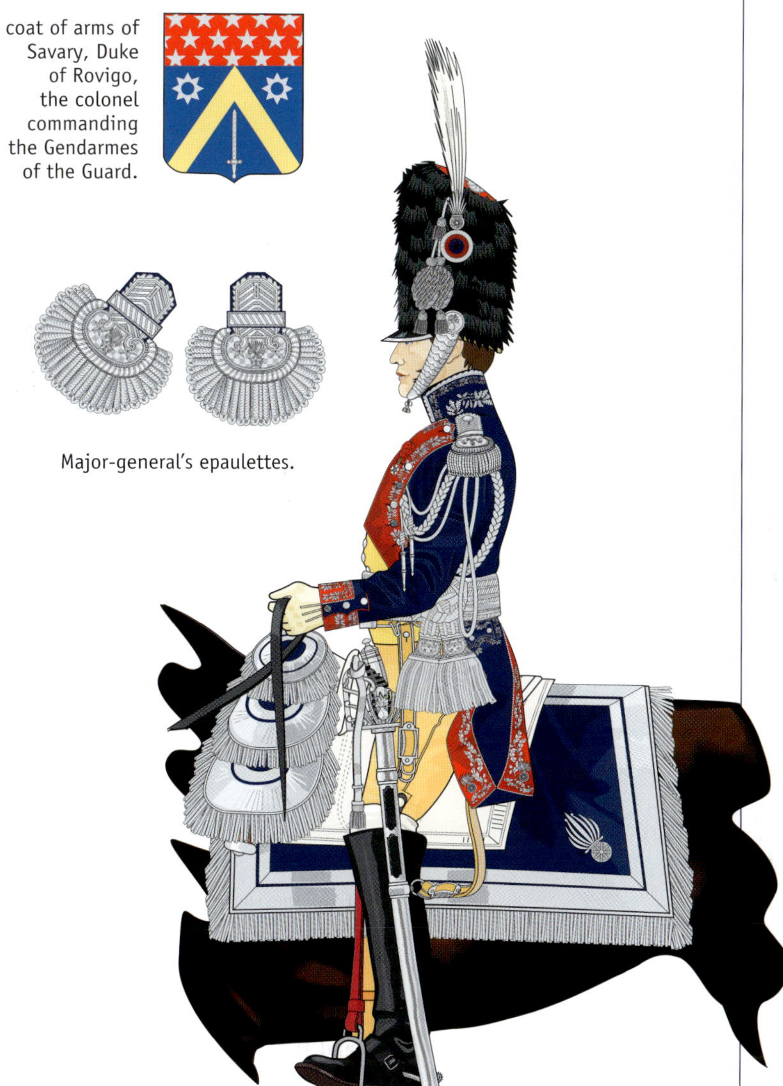

THE GENDARMERIE D'ELITE

The Headquarters
1 Colonel
1 Major
2 Squadron Commanders (one on foot)
1 Quartermaster
1 Adjudant-major
2 Under Adjudant-majors (one on foot)
2 Health Officers
2 Standard-bearers
1 Flag-Bearer
1 Veterinary Officer
12 musicians
1 Master-Saddler
1 Master-Tailor and Gaiter maker
1 Master-Breech-maker
1 Master-Boot-maker
1 Master-Armourer and Spur-maker

Each Mounted squadrons
First-Lieutenants
1 Marechal-des-logis Chef
1 Marechal-des-logis
1 Fourrier
6 Brigadiers
72 Gendarmes
2 Trumpeters
1 Blacksmith

quarters dress and for town dress. The coat with a cape and sleeves was imperial blue and had three buttonholes with white braid. Stable dress comprised a jacket with two rows of cloth buttons and fatigue trousers.

From 1801 to 1804 the Gendarmes wore a black felt hat trimmed with white braid; the braid of the cockade and the curl tied with ribbon with a fringe were also silver. In full dress, the hat had a scarlet plume. They were also issued with a second hat for service dress. A blue forage cap with red frogs and a tassel made of white thread; the headband was decorated with two white stripes and a grenade made of white cloth.

In 1806 a black bearskin hat with a visor and strap replaced the hat; the outer reinforcement of the visor and the scales on the chinstrap were made of white metal. The scarlet background was decorated with a white grenade.

A red (or white depending on the period) plume, a tricolour pompon-cockade and a simple cord made of white thread, with two flounders and three tassels completed the hat.

Between 1804 and 1808-1809, the Gendarmes à Cheval used semi-stiff boots with knee pieces for parade dress; then they were given stiff boots with smooth calves.

For ordinary service dress they were given soft boots. The spurs were made of blackened iron. For quarters or exercise dress they wore a pair of gaiters.

The Equipment

The belt, the cartridge-case shoulder-strap and the musket shoulder-belt were made of yellowed hide and edged with a white thread braid; all the rest of the strappings were yellow. The belt-plate decorated with

A platoon of Gendarmes d'Elite of the Imperial Guard escorting prisoners from Moscow during the great fire in December 1812.
(Oil painting by Victor Huen, "la Grande Armee", Private collection, RR).

an embossed grenade was made of brass. The gauntlets were yellow ochre. The flap of the cartridge case was made of black leather but its exact shape is not known but it was decorated with a yellow brass grenade; it was replaced in 1806 by a crowned eagle.

The Weapons

The Gendarmes à Cheval were issued with a sabre and a pair of pistols, the Gendarmes à Pied with an infantry sabre; all of them were armed with a carbine and a bayonet.

The sabre with a straight-edged blade was that of the Cavalry of the Line, first the An IX model then the An XIII model with an iron scabbard. In about 1806-07 the Gendarmerie d'Elite received the Guards Grenadiers à Cheval sabre.

The pistols were first the An-IX model then the An XIII model. Various carbine models were used: at the beginning of the Empire, the Gendarmes still used the cavalry's 1763-1766 carbine or the mounted police's 1770-model carbine; they were then issued with the An-IX then the An-XIII models

The Harnesses

The French-style of harness was used; the saddle and the holsters were made of tawny leather; all the leather was black and the buckles were made of brass. The studs of the bridle bit were stamped with a grenade. The saddlecloth and the flaps were made of dark blue cloth.

The tips were decorated with a grenade made of white thread; this was replaced by a crown in 1807. In full dress, the white fillet replaced the black fillet.

The portmanteau was rectangular not round and made of blue cloth; its ends had white braid. Up to 1807, a similarly-shaped bag was placed on top of the portmanteau; it was held in place by a long flap on the portmanteau which covered and held everything in place.

The coat was folded over like a wallet with the lining showing and was placed on top of the portmanteau and bag.

The ends of the portmanteaux issued after 1807 had double white braid.

THE GENDARME D'ELITE

Considering them apart and not taking into account his position in the Guard, the Gendarme d'Elite could be mistaken for a Grenadier à cheval; there was almost the same serious look; moreover, under the visor descending from his bearskin onto his eyebrows, you could see the penetrating look of a soldier invested with a mission of trust shining out at you; there was something of the inquisition and of suspicion in his unceasingly worried look.

He always seemed on the qui-vive and his watchfulness was rarely caught out. This was because his job was to watch over the safety of the Emperor in person; he was the indispensable soldier for imperial residences; it was he who made sure the sovereign's ordnances were respected and carried out, and who detained bodily, whatever their rank or their position the army, all the wrongdoers risking their Master's severity or disgrace. Although the Gendarme d'Elite was more or less the General Headquarters' policeman, he fought nonetheless in the ranks of the Old Guard when on the battlefield."

Marco de Saint-Hilaire Histoire de la Garde imperiale.

The Gendarmerie d'Elite

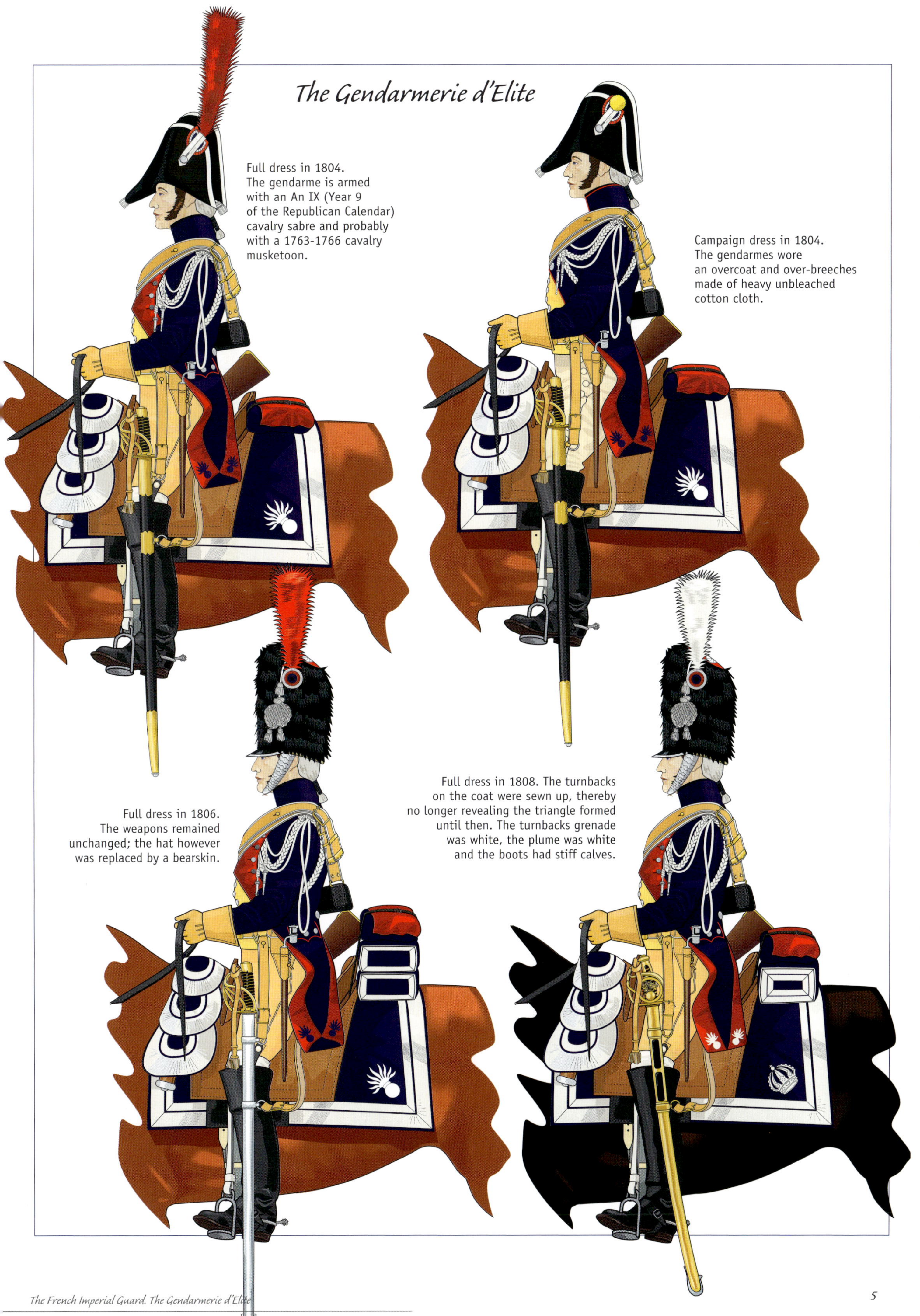

Full dress in 1804.
The gendarme is armed with an An IX (Year 9 of the Republican Calendar) cavalry sabre and probably with a 1763-1766 cavalry musketoon.

Campaign dress in 1804.
The gendarmes wore an overcoat and over-breeches made of heavy unbleached cotton cloth.

Full dress in 1806.
The weapons remained unchanged; the hat however was replaced by a bearskin.

Full dress in 1808. The turnbacks on the coat were sewn up, thereby no longer revealing the triangle formed until then. The turnbacks grenade was white, the plume was white and the boots had stiff calves.

Campaign dress

The gendarmes «bis» created in 1813 were part of the Young Guard. They wore the same dress as the Old Guard but did not have an overcoat; the bearskin had no decorations.

Campaign dress in about 1813-1814.

Campaign dress in about 1808.

Full service dress on foot 1807-1814.

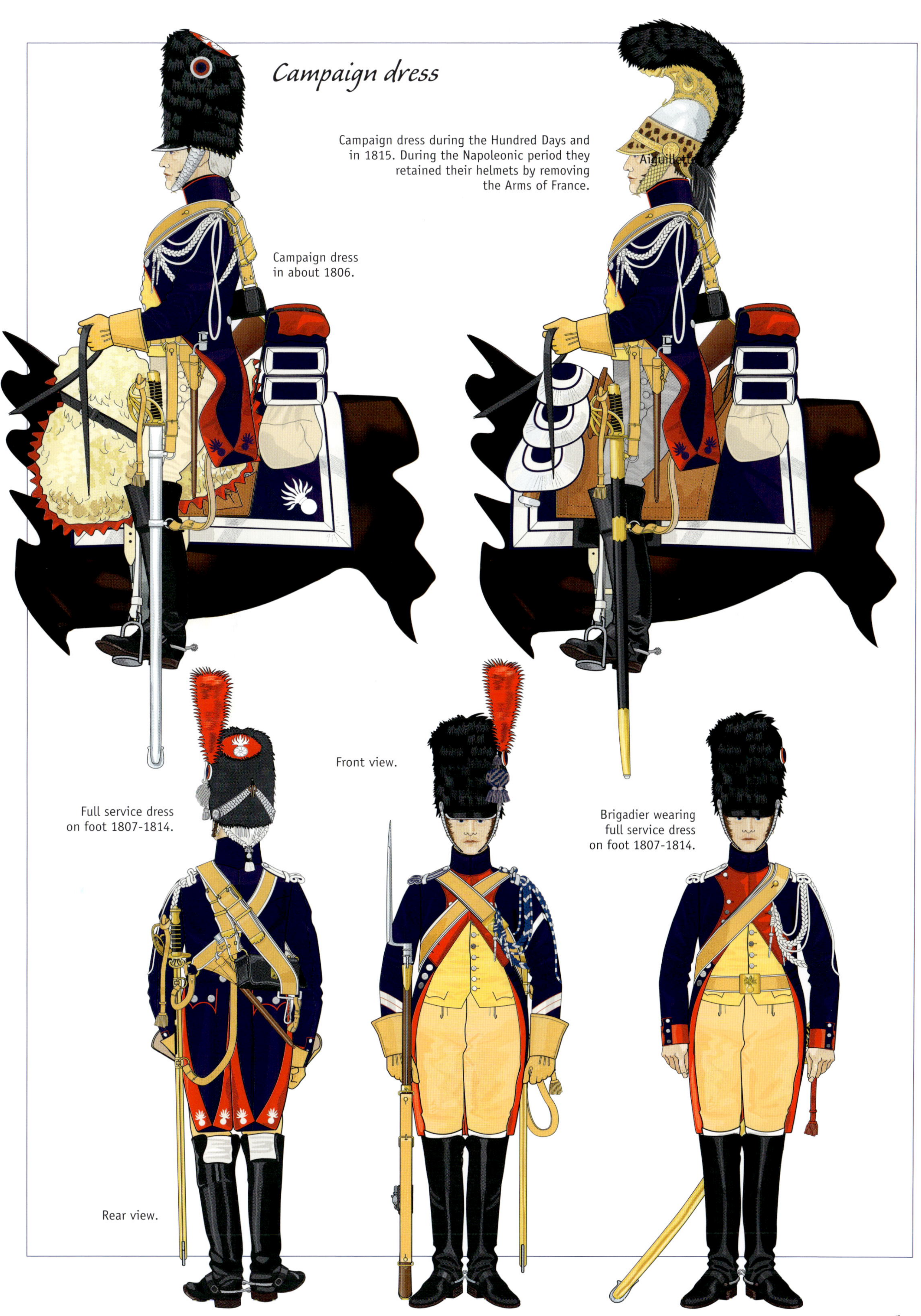
Campaign dress
Campaign dress during the Hundred Days and in 1815. During the Napoleonic period they retained their helmets by removing the Arms of France.
Aiguillette
Campaign dress in about 1806.
Front view.
Full service dress on foot 1807-1814.
Brigadier wearing full service dress on foot 1807-1814.
Rear view.

Garde's dress,
wearing
an overcoat,
1807-1814.
Gendarme «bis»
in 1813.
Social dress.
The Gendarmerie d'Elite
Gendarme wearing
a coat, 1804.
Social dress
wearing
an overcoat.
Garde's dress,
wearing
an overcoat.
Service dress,
wearing an overcoat.

The Trumpeters

Trumpeter wearing an overcoat in about 1804, according to Commandant Bucquoy's card collection.

Trumpeter wearing an overcoat in about 1806, in service with the Emperor.

Trumpeter wearing full dress in about 1807, after P. Begnini.

Trumpeter in campaign dress in about 1804-1806, after P. Begnini.

The Trumpeters

Trumpeter in full dress about 1804-1806, after P. Begnini.

Trumpeter in campaign dress.

Musician wearing full dress in about 1810, according to drawing from the Alsatian Collections.

Trumpeter wearing full dress, during the Hundred Days.

Trumpeter in Full parade dress

Trumpetter in full dress, 1806-1814, by Begnini.
(Private Collection, RR)

Trumpeter wearing full parade dress in about 1806, after Hoffmann.

The Timpanist

According to an engraving by n,
the timpanist is wearing a coat with a red collar and a red timpanist's apron with three silver stripes around the edge.
He is riding a bay.

A timpanist, according to the set of plates by Noirmont and Marbot.

A timpanist, according to Plate N°6 "le Plumet" by Rigo.

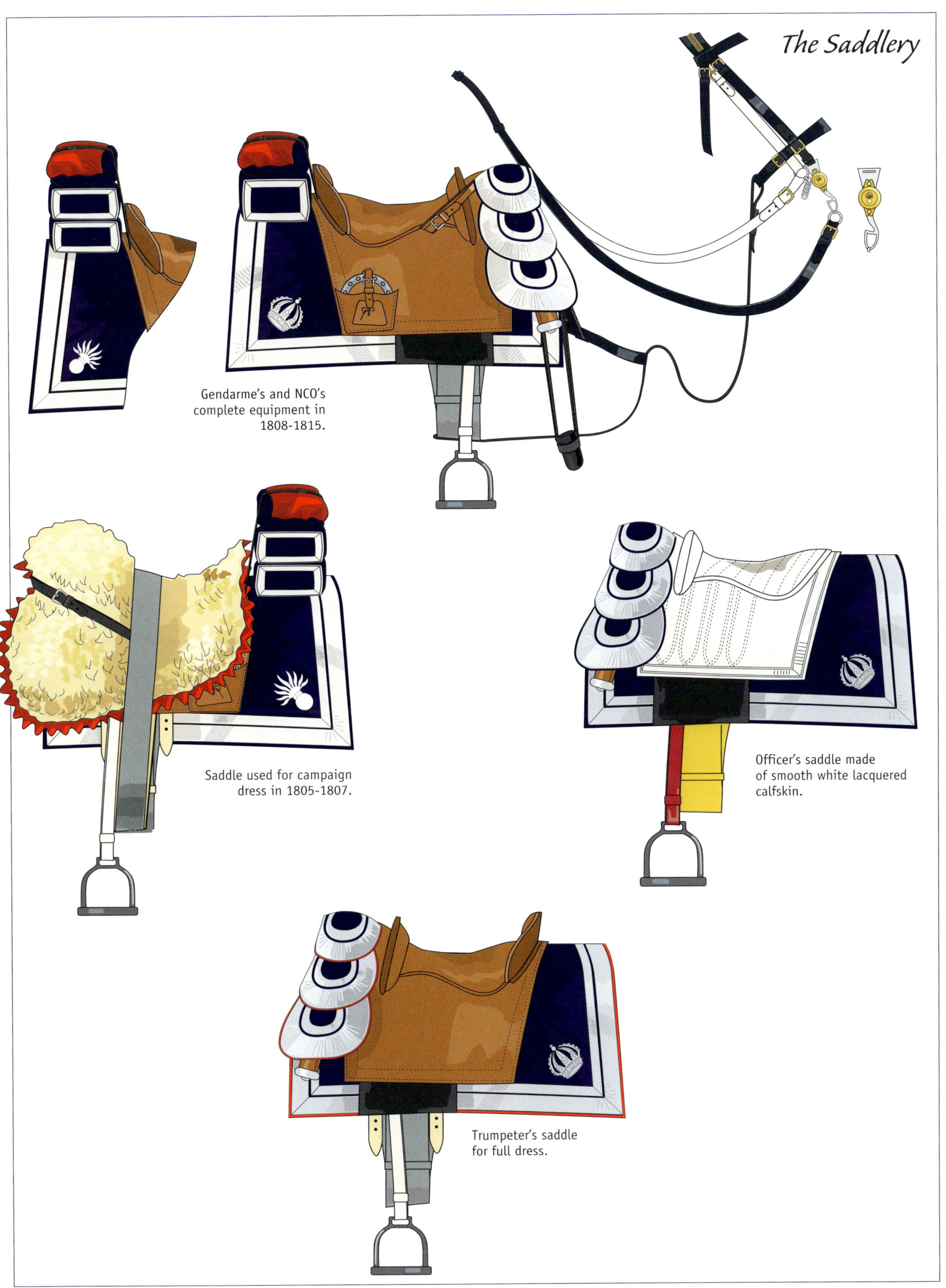

Gendarme's and NCO's complete equipment in 1808-1815.

Saddle used for campaign dress in 1805-1807.

Officer's saddle made of smooth white lacquered calfskin.

Trumpeter's saddle for full dress.

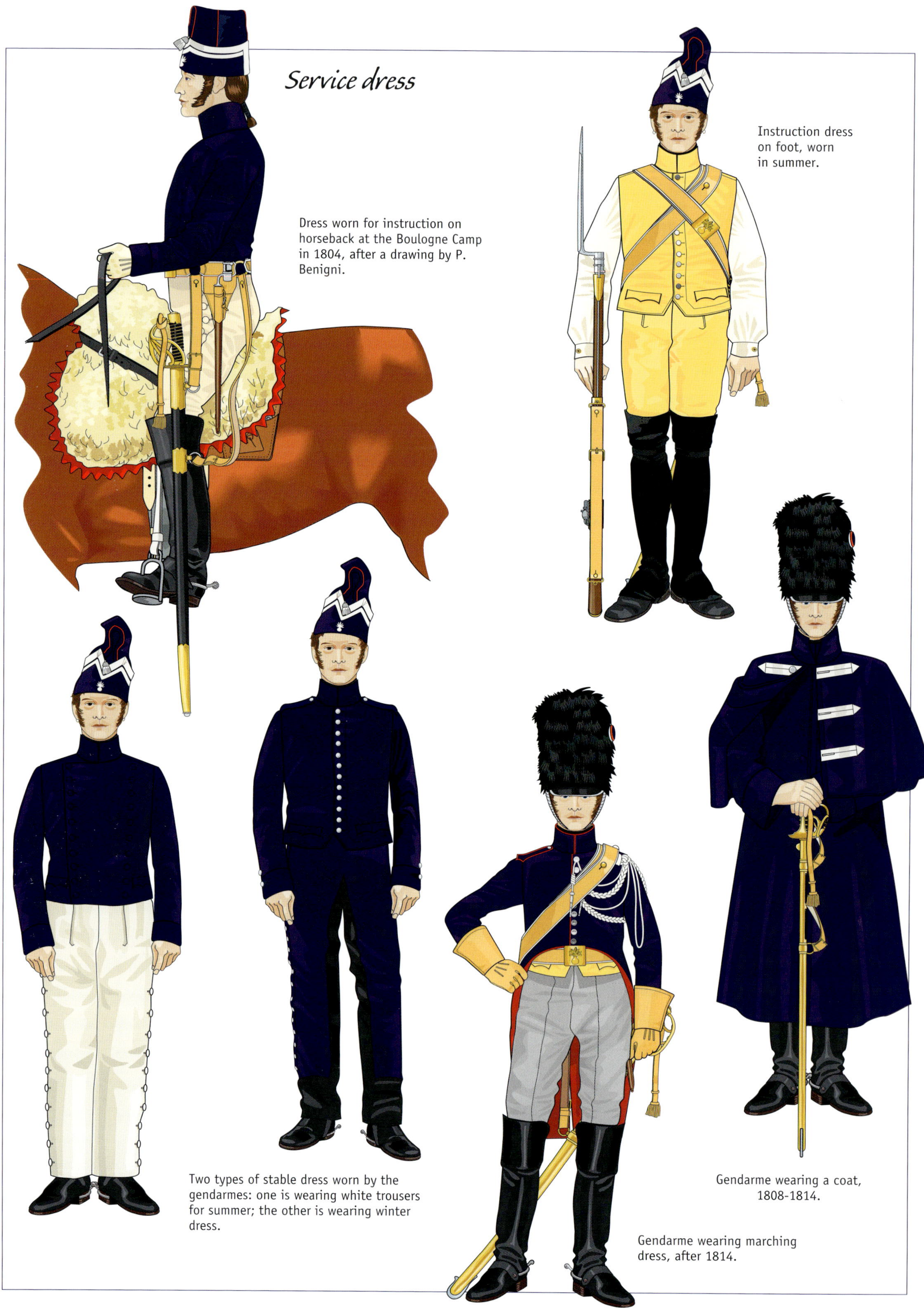

Service dress

Dress worn for instruction on horseback at the Boulogne Camp in 1804, after a drawing by P. Benigni.

Instruction dress on foot, worn in summer.

Two types of stable dress worn by the gendarmes: one is wearing white trousers for summer; the other is wearing winter dress.

Gendarme wearing a coat, 1808-1814.

Gendarme wearing marching dress, after 1814.

Gendarme's coat in 1804-1808 and 1808-1814 the difference lies in the way the turnbacks are positioned in another manner.

Overcoat.

Flat uniform button.

The gendarmes d'elite uniform

Waistcoat.

Gendarme's white and silver forage cap for the NCOs.

Boot sleeve made of stiff cloth. It was used to protect the breeches from wear and tear caused by the boots rubbing.

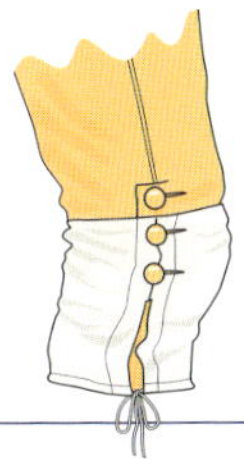

Brigadier.

Marechal-des-logis.

Marechal-des-logis chef.

Breeches.

The NCOs

Marechal des logis wearing full dress, 1808-1814.

Marechal des logis wearing full dress, 1808-1814.

Marechal des logis wearing full dress, 1806-1808.

Brigadier wearing town dress, 1807-1814.

Brigadier wearing guard dress, in 1804.

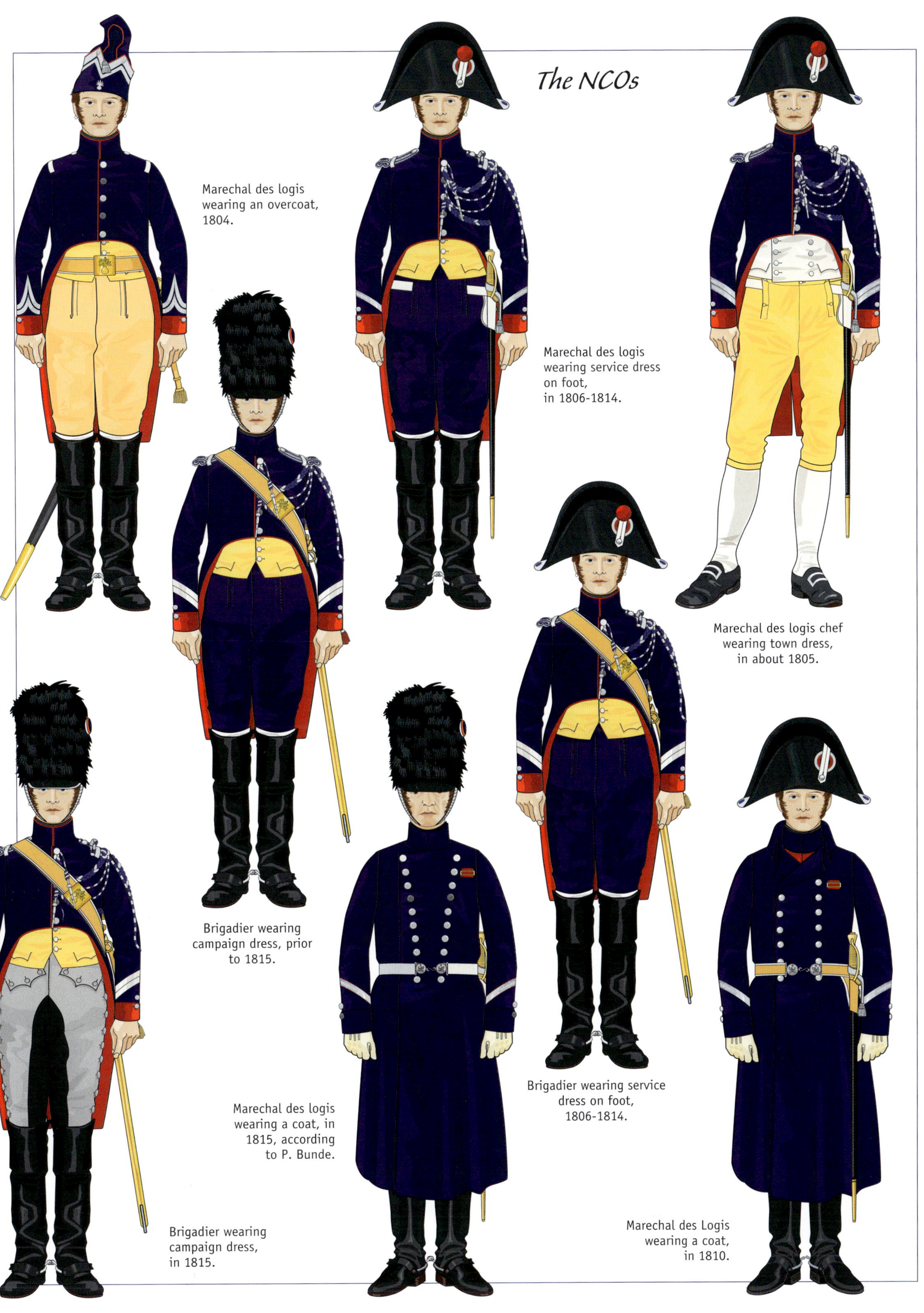
The NCOs
Marechal des logis
wearing an overcoat,
1804.
Marechal des logis
wearing service dress
on foot,
in 1806-1814.
Marechal des logis chef
wearing town dress,
in about 1805.
Brigadier wearing
campaign dress, prior
to 1815.
Brigadier wearing service
dress on foot,
1806-1814.
Marechal des logis
wearing a coat, in
1815, according
to P. Bunde.
Brigadier wearing
campaign dress,
in 1815.
Marechal des Logis
wearing a coat,
in 1810.

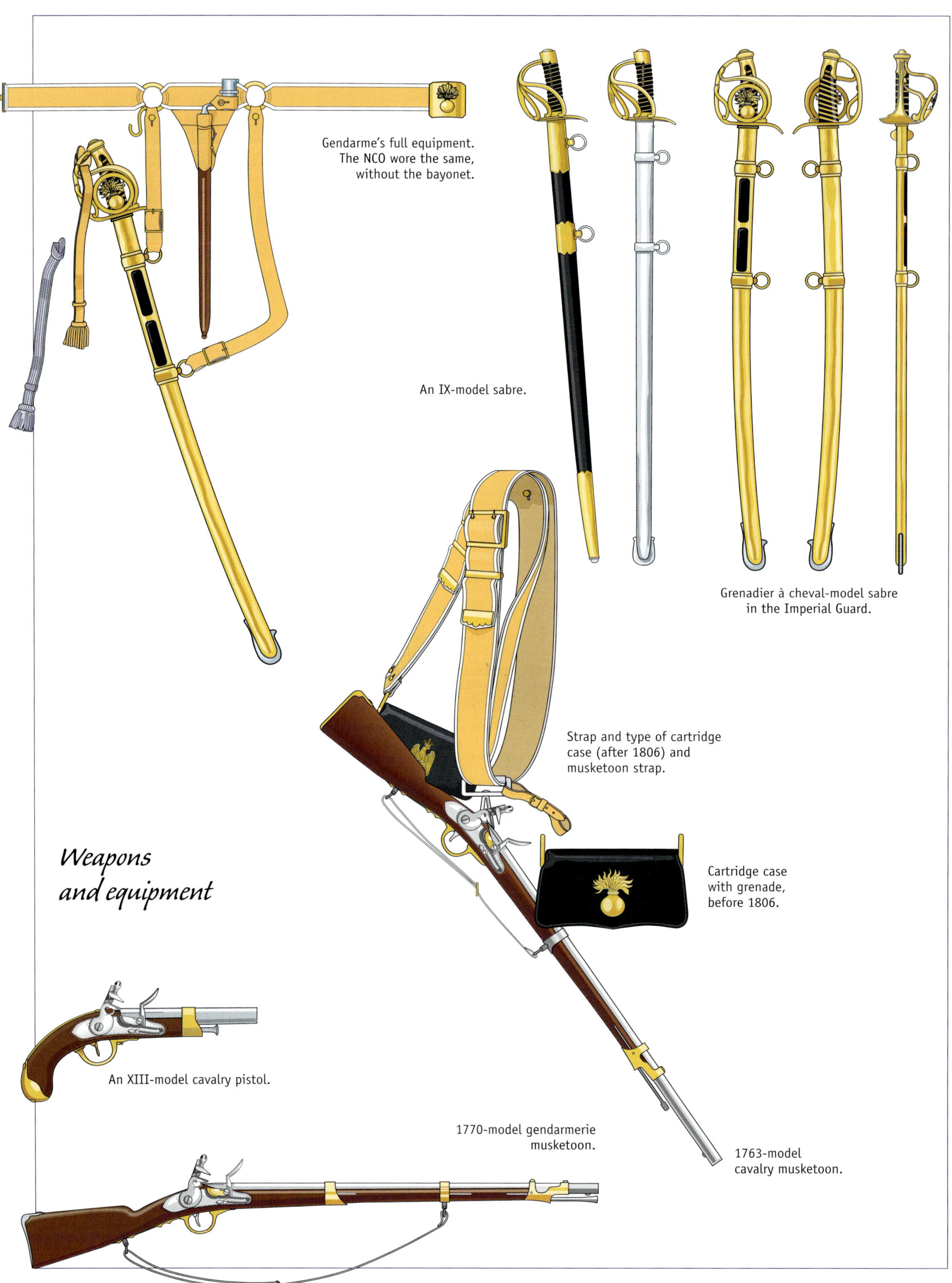

Weapons and equipment

The Gendarmerie d'Elite Officers

Officer wearing an overcoat for the service on foot.

Officer wearing full service dress, during the whole of the Empire.

Officer wearing social dress.

Officer wearing a coat, in about 1808.

Officer, mounted, from the foot company.

The Gendarmerie d'Elite Officers

Officer wearing an overcoat in exercise dress in about 1810, according to a drawing by P. Begnini.

Surgeon wearing an overcoat. *A reconstitution attempt.*

Officer wearing an overcoat for town dress.

Officer wearing an overcoat for service dress.

On 24 September 1806, the Emperor sent a letter to the Minister of the Interior: *"Monsieur Champagny, you will find attached an idea for a circular which you can set out as you wish. You will communicate it to Minister Dejean so that he can send it to Marechal Kellermann"* The project he had in mind was to recruit and set up a new corps, the Gendarmes d'Ordonnance.

Napoleon continued: *"I do not know what will come of it. You know that I do not need troops, but I do wish to open up this career again to all those who have been cut off from their motherland by the circumstances of the Revolution; after all, it is such a natural career for any Frenchman. If you adopt these measures, you will have to write immediately to the Prefects of Paris and the neighbouring departments."*

It is easy to understand that the idea behind this was political: an attempt by Napoleon to attract the sons of emigre families which had returned to France. He entertained the hope that he would be able to make them into an elite unit for his household, even to re-establish the *Compagnies de Gardes du corps* (Life Guard Companies) as they were under the *Ancien Regime*.

The reasons for him doing this were confirmed in a letter addressed to Marechal Kellermann on 25 October 1806: "[...] *By organising this corps, I have been influenced more by political than by military considerations* [...]".

He also stipulated what the entry conditions were and how the corps was to be organised. "[...] *Any man between 18 and 40, who has enough money to buy his own equipment, to buy a horse and go to Mainz and contact Marechal Kellermann. He will be admitted into the Emperor's Gendarmes d'Ordonnance.*

Marechal Kellermann has been given all the powers he needs to organise companies of 80 men and to appoint the officers from among those who have already served and who have the necessary qualities [...]."

As soon as the circular was distributed, the old aristocracy flocked to Mainz to join this new elite corps, the *Gendarmes d'Ordonnance de la Maison de l'Empereur*. By November, Marechal Kellermann was able to set up the first two companies (there were to be six); they were organised in the same way as the Chasseurs à Cheval of the Guard.

The uniform was designed by General Lacune and made official in the regulation dated October 1806. It was green with white buttons, without a distinctive colour but with silver striping.

The simple horseman looked just like an officer! They were very quickly the envy of the rest of the Guard who thought they were too privileged

The 135-strong 1st Company was under the command of the Comte de Montmorency-Laval; it was detached from the army and arrived in Berlin on 13 December. The 2nd Company with 150 men was under the orders of the Comte d'Arberg but only joined the army in January 1807. The 3rd and 4th Companies were only operational by April and May 1807. As for the 5th Company, its existence, like that of the Foot Company, was all too brief.

Indeed, only the first three companies took part in the 1807 campaign; the other two stayed in Berlin. First used to pursue Major von Schill's partisans, the Gendarmes d'Ordonnance then fought alongside the Italian division under General Teulie and made a name for themselves in several engagements: their conduct at Kolberg even got their name into the 63rd and 69th Grande Armee Bulletins.

At the beginning of April 1807, they reached Marienwerder where they served with the Emperor who reviewed them. Satisfied by their behaviour, he awarded seven Croix of the Legion d'Honneur. Then after several other engagements they took part in the battle of Friedland, on 14 June.

The peace treaty was signed at Tilsit on 25 June followed by a lot of festivities during which the troops fraternised. During a banquet offered to the Russian Imperial Guard by the French Imperial Guard, the Gendarmes d'Ordonnance found themselves among some of their former fellow emigres. Given the task of hosting the Chevaliers-Gardes, they drank and raised their glasses to the former King's Household: the aristocracy had not forgotten the Ancien Regime.

This behaviour was not exactly to the liking of the rest of the French Imperial Guard and the senior officers. It was perhaps one of the reasons that hastened this corps' demise: at Koensigberg, the Gendarmes d'Ordonnance paraded on 12 July 1807, in front of Marechal Bessières who told them they were to be disbanded.

The final decree dated the following 23 October showed that the Emperor had not forgotten the services they had rendered: *"The companies of Gendarmes d'Ordonnance of our Guard are to be disbanded; however, in order to show how much we are satisfied with their service, we will admit the Gendarmes who followed the last campaign into the chasseurs, grenadiers and dragoons à cheval of our Guard. As for the others they will join the Line or the Velites."*

The Gendarmes d'Ordonnance had to pay for their own equipment and uniforms.

Although the dress was simple and rather strict-looking, the equipment on the other hand was very luxurious and, according to Lieutenant de Norvins cost a packet!

The shako

This was the 1806 model, made of black felt decorated with a black velvet stripe. The visor was made of leather with a silver metal edging. The plate was an all-silver lozenge with a stamped, crowned eagle.

Contemporary sources show that there were variants. The cord was silver braid with two flounders. The chinstrap consisted of silver metal scales.

The tricolour cockade was held in place by double silver loop and a silver button. The whole was surmounted by a white plume.

The Coat

This was a green "à la chasseur" coat with pointed facings and lapels, just like those worn by the Chasseurs à Cheval of the Guard but much more austere; there was no distinctive.

(Continued on page 26)

The Gendarmes d'ordonnance

Gendarme d'Ordonnance wearing full dress in 1807, according to H. Boisselier

Gendarme d'Ordonnance wearing full dress in 1807, according to Kolbe.

Gendarme d'Ordonnance wearing full dress in 1807, according to Henschel.

Gendarme d'Ordonnance wearing full dress in 1807, according to H. Boisselier, rear and front views.

Gendarme d'Ordonnance wearing full dress in 1807, according to Noirmont and Marbot.

The Gendarmes d'ordonnance

Officer wearing full dress in 1807, according to the Alsatian Collections.

NCO wearing full dress in 1807 according to the Alsatian Collections. Note that the hat has no cockade.

Gendarme d'Ordonnance wearing full dress in 1807, according to Weiland.

Gendarme in marching dress, 1807.

Gendarme in a frock coat, according to the Alsatian Collections.

Gendarme wearing a coat, according to the Alsatian Collections.

Gendarme wearing a cloak-coat with sleeves, according to H. Boisselier

Gendarme wearing marching dress or escort picket, after a drawing by P. Courcelle.

The Trumpeters

Trumpeter, according to the Strasbourg collection of little soldiers.

Trumpeter, according to Plate n°176 of "le Plumet".

Trumpeter, according to H. Boisselier.

Buttons

Waistcoat.

Breeches.

Trumpeter's coat.

The gendarmes and trumpeters uniforms

(continued from page 21)

The turnbacks were attached with a button; the pockets were tailored "à la Soubise". The round buttons were silver; flat buttons, with a stamped eagle, might also have been used.

The Aiglet

This was the Guards' model. It was silver braid cord for the troopers and the officers. Although no document confirms this, it must be supposed that the silver NCO aiglet was mixed with green silk.

Although there is no controversy over the Gendarmes d'Ordonnance belonging to the Guard, period documentary evidence on the other hand does show that they wore aiglets; but these were sometimes worn on the right, and sometimes on the left... it depends on the source.

The Waistcoat

This was tailored à la hongroise and was made of scarlet cashmere, decorated with silver buttons and three rows of round silver buttons.

For the NCOs the same can be said as for the aiglets: the braid may have been mixed with green silk.

The Breeches and The Riding Breeches

These were Hungarian-style breeches lade of green cloth decorated with a silver stripe down the side and two Hungarian knots on the front that were sometimes replaced by a single stripe and shaped into an inverted point.

The riding breeches or "charivari" were made of green cloth. The inner leg was lined with green cloth or blackened sheepskin. The sides were fastened with buttons and the stripe was identical to that of the breeches.

The Equipment

This consisted of the cartridge case and its strap, a carbine belt and a belt. All this black leather-work was varnished and had silver stitching. Some documents show the leatherwork with scarlet stitches. All the buckles were silver coloured. The cartridge case had a plate like the one on the shako. There was a stamped eagle attached to a pin decorating the front of its strap. The whole was silver-coloured.

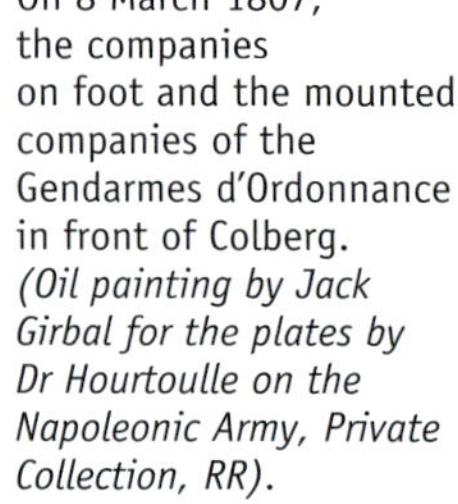

On 8 March 1807, the companies on foot and the mounted companies of the Gendarmes d'Ordonnance in front of Colberg. *(Oil painting by Jack Girbal for the plates by Dr Hourtoulle on the Napoleonic Army, Private Collection, RR).*

The Weapons

As the Gendarmes d'Ordonnance were organised like the Chasseurs à Cheval of the Guard, they should have been armed with the 1786-model carbine but nothing is less certain, and the pistol should have been the AN-XIII model, but no document confirms this.

The Harnesses

This was in the Hungarian style. The leather was black and the buckles were silver. The schabrack was made of green cloth decorated with a silver stripe and scarlet piping. The corners were embroidered with a silver eagle.

The portmanteau had silver striping.

The Marks of Rank

The only things that distinguished the officers from the troopers were the one or two silver epaulettes and the width of the stripes.

There are no reliable sources for the senior officers or the NCOs.

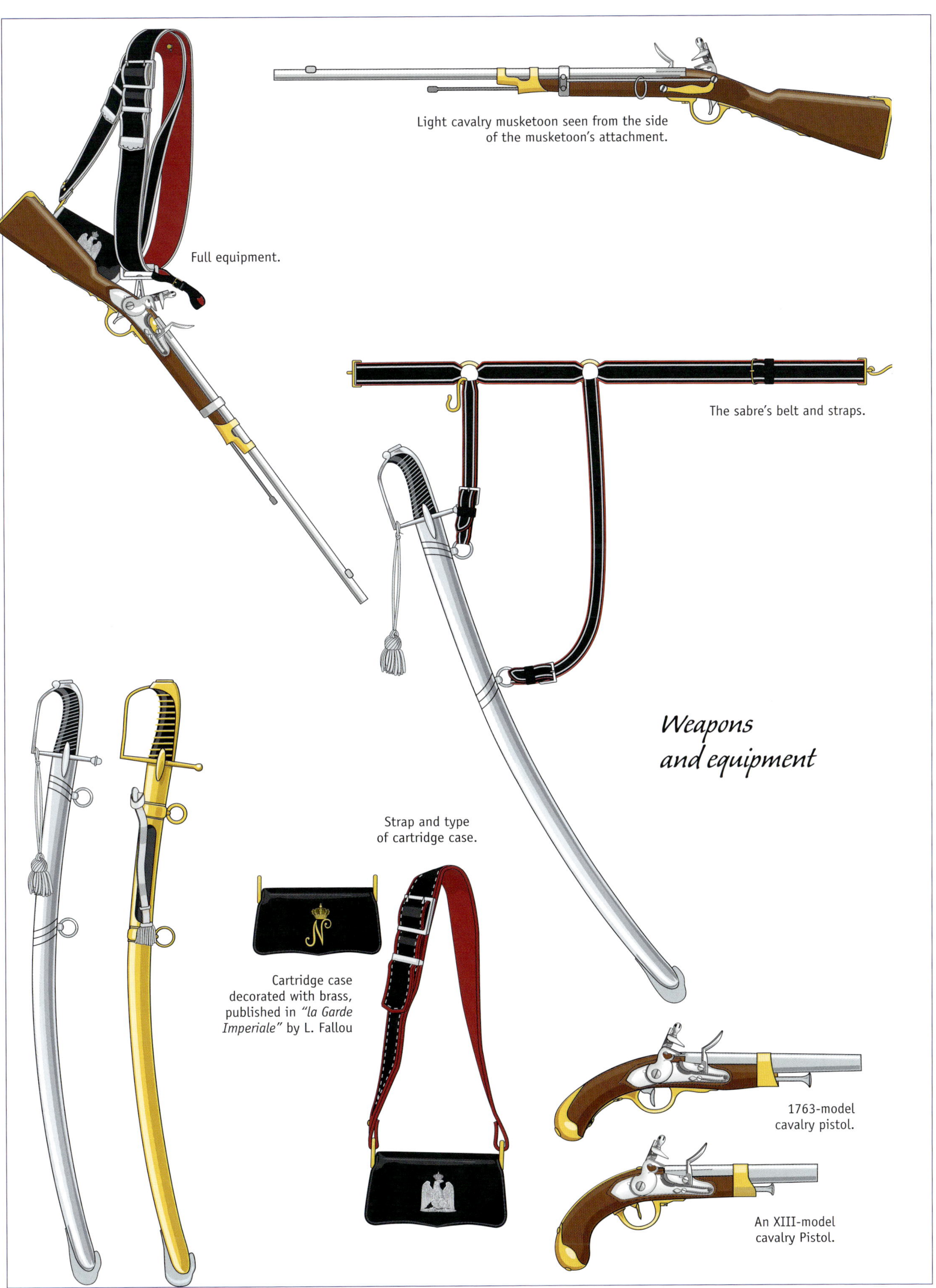
Light cavalry musketoon seen from the side
of the musketoon's attachment.
Full equipment.
The sabre's belt and straps.
Weapons
and equipment
Strap and type
of cartridge case.
Cartridge case
decorated with brass,
published in *"la Garde
Imperiale"* by L. Fallou
1763-model
cavalry pistol.
An XIII-model
cavalry Pistol.

The chasseurs à cheval squadrons of the Young Guard

When he returned from Russia, the Emperor created four new two-company squadrons (the 11th to the 18th) in the Chasseurs à Cheval.

The Squadrons of the so-called Young Guard

In 1813 and 1814, the 6th, 7th, 8th and 9th squadrons, called the Young Guard, took part in the German Campaign and they fought especially in France alongside their elders and the cavalrymen of the three regiments of scouts. During the Restoration, with the cuts in numbers which were planned as the Corps Royal des Chasseurs de France were being formed, these troopers deserted *"en masse"*, or were transferred to the cavalry regiments of the Line, havens and regiments which they did not hesitate to abandon when Napoleon returned from exile and recreated the Cavalry of the Guard.

The 2nd chasseurs à cheval regiment

Napoleon decided to reinforce the cavalry of the Guard significantly on 15 May 1815, and the Emperor therefore created a new regiment of light cavalry, called first of all the *Tirailleurs de la Garde*, then *Hussards-Eclaireurs de la Jeune Garde*.

The administration of the regiment was taken over by the Chasseurs à Cheval of the Guard's administration.

On May 26, having almost got back up to strength again, the ephemeral Hussars of the Guard were finally given the name of the Second Regiment of Chasseurs à Cheval of the Guard. Lieutenant-General Lefebvre-Desnouettes, who was a weapons inspector for the Light Cavalry of the Guard, was above all a colonel in the Chasseurs of the Old Guard, so he became the Colonel of the new regiment, leaving Marechal de Camp Marlin de Douai to take command of the regiment with the rank of Major in the Old Guard.

Having replaced the 1st Chasseurs à Cheval Regiment in Paris, the regiment did not take part in the Belgian Campaign and was not present at the disaster at Waterloo. Their loyalty to the Emperor caused them countless problems with the King's partisans in the first days of the summer of 1815.

Recruitment

The troopers in the regiment came mainly from the oldest regiments in the Guards (Chasseurs à Cheval, Dragoons, Grenadiers and Lancers) or from the regiments of the Line which had to hand over troopers with four years' service or campaigning.

The troopers coming from the Line were mainly former Chasseurs in the Young Guard squadrons who had seen sent to these same regiments of the Line a year earlier.

This was the rather torturous path which Captain Parquin, the famous memorialist followed after 1813, the year when he was a Lieutenant in the 11th Company of the Young Guard, before being promoted to Captain of Cuirassiers in 1814.

He returned to the Second Regiment of the Chasseurs à Cheval of the Guard in 1815.

Regimental strength

A few days after its incorporation, the Second Regiment of Chasseurs à Cheval of the Guards numbered 27 officers for 709 troopers with its four squadrons and headquarters.

At the time when the Chasseurs à Cheval of the Old Guard fought at Waterloo, the regiment numbered 53 officers and 921 troopers.

In July there were only 35 officers and 640 troopers and NCOs.

When it was finally disbanded, the regimental rolls listed only 40 officers and 266 troopers.

Uniform and equipment

The Young Guard squadrons wore the same items of clothing, dolman, belt, waistcoat and breeches as their brothers-in-arms in the Old Guard. When the unit was created, the shako used was the 1812 model, although no document confirms this hypothesis. The leatherwork was not stitched.

According to Lefebvre-Desnouettes' description, the chasseurs and the NCOs received a madder brown shako-rouleau with a double visor, tresses and green and aurora cockade braid. The shako cord was yellow for the troopers and plaited green and yellow for the NCOs. The hat issued to the chasseurs in the Second Regiment was the one attributed to the Chasseurs of the 1st Regiment.

The forage cap was green and was made and ornamented in the same way as the one worn by the Old Guard.

Although the dolman was described as being green and having aurora tresses and loops, a green collar and bright red facings, it was never issued. The belts were green with bright red knots but they were not issued either.

The pelisse was theoretically bright red with tresses and yellow braid. The fur was black. It seems however that pelisses intended for the Old Guard were diverted to the benefit of the Second Regiment.

The breeches were not intended to be Hungarian style. The riding breeches were green with two bright red stripes. In fact, trousers with a bright red stripe were the only ones worn.

The sabre was the An-XI model with a branch mounting. The pistol and the carbine with a bayonet were identical to those used by the Old Guard.

The saddle was the hussars', covered with a schabrack with a white sheepskin seat, with no ornamentation in the lower corners.

The officers and the NCOs retained the Chasseurs à Cheval's dress and weapons since they had come from that regiments' war squadrons.

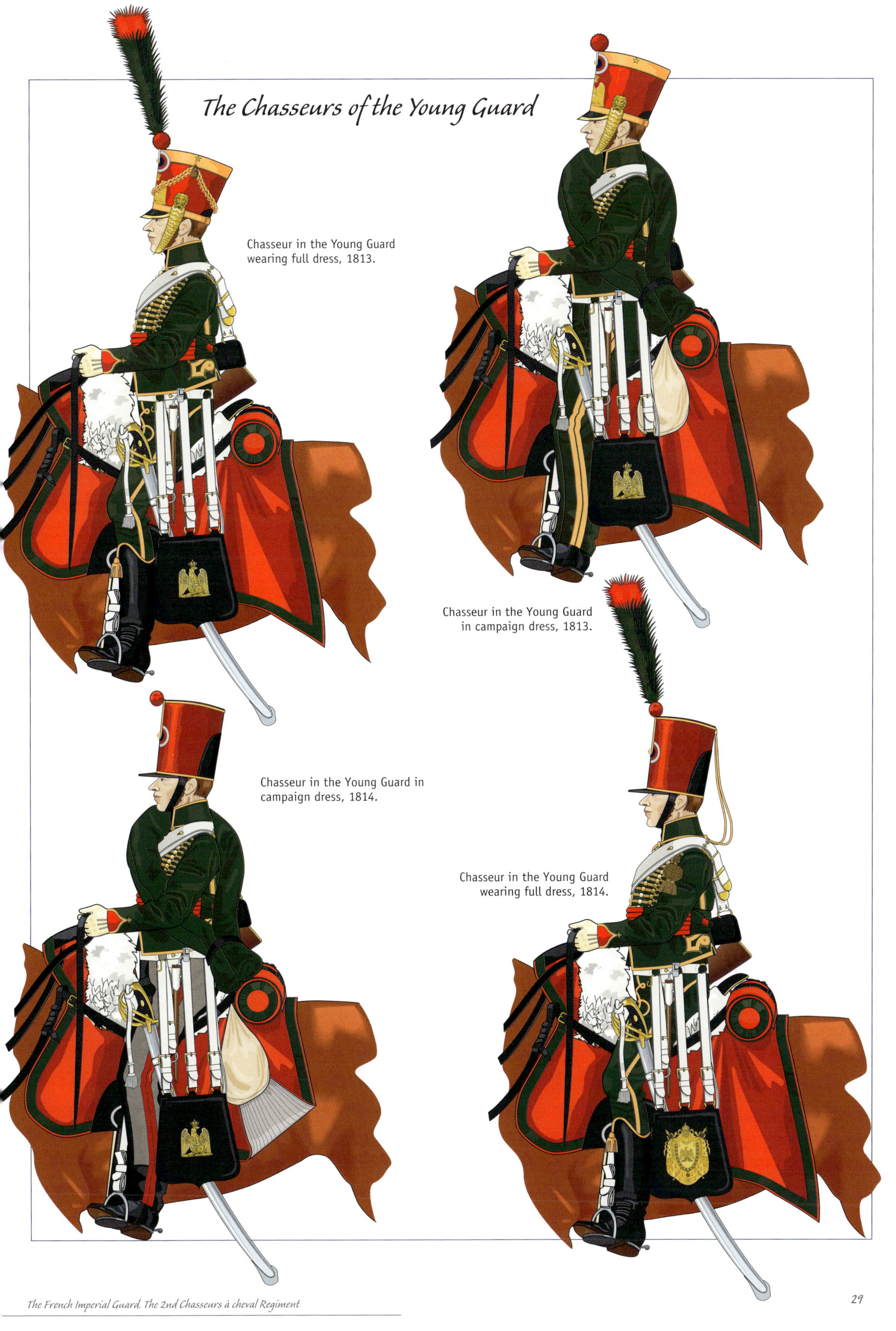

The Chasseurs of the Young Guard

Chasseur in the Young Guard wearing full dress, 1813.

Chasseur in the Young Guard in campaign dress, 1813.

Chasseur in the Young Guard in campaign dress, 1814.

Chasseur in the Young Guard wearing full dress, 1814.

The Chasseurs of the Young Guard

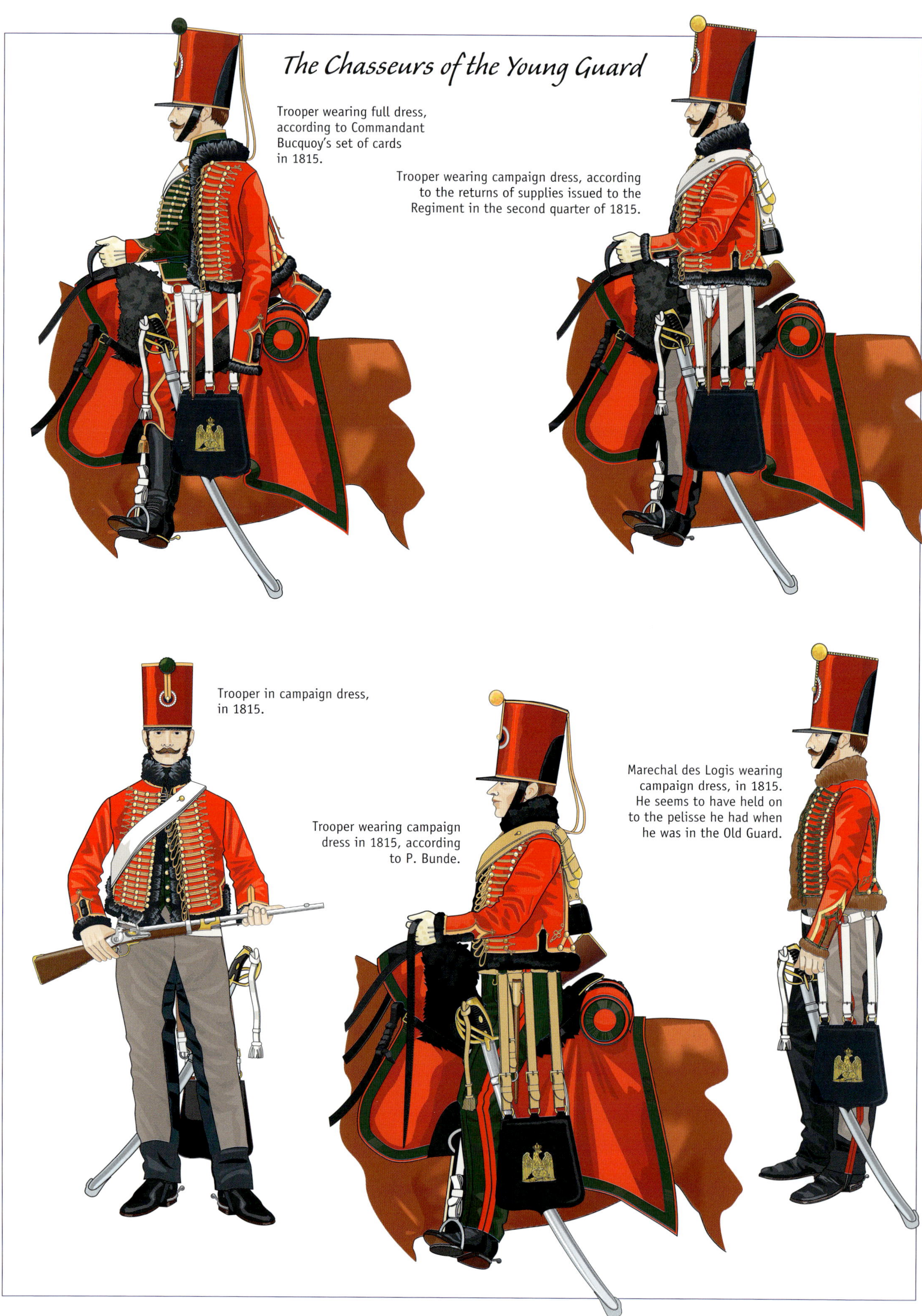

Trooper wearing full dress, according to Commandant Bucquoy's set of cards in 1815.

Trooper wearing campaign dress, according to the returns of supplies issued to the Regiment in the second quarter of 1815.

Trooper in campaign dress, in 1815.

Trooper wearing campaign dress in 1815, according to P. Bunde.

Marechal des Logis wearing campaign dress, in 1815. He seems to have held on to the pelisse he had when he was in the Old Guard.

The 2nd Chasseurs Regiment

Trooper wearing full dress at the time the Regiment was created.

Trooper wearing campaign dress with the shako-rouleau in its protective sheath, and riding breeches.

Trooper in campaign dress in 1815.

Trooper in campaign dress in 1815 with grey "charivari".

Trooper wearing campaign dress, side view, in 1815.

Trooper wearing a cloak coat with sleeves and rotunda cape.

The 2nd Chasseurs Trumpeters

Trumpeter wearing campaign dress in 1815 according to the old Ministry of Defence archives.

Trumpeter wearing marching dress in 1815.

Trumpeter, according to the Alsatian Collections.

An other trumpeter, according to the Alsatian Collections.

The 2nd Chasseurs Trumpeters

Trumpeter from the 2nd Chasseur à cheval Regiment, wearing campaign dress.

Trumpet-major in 1815, as described by H. Boisselier.

A variant of the trumpet-major in 1815.

Trumpeter-major in campaign dress in 1815 wearing a jacket, according to H. Boisselier.

The Officers of the 2nd Chasseurs à cheval Regiment

Officers in 1815, wearing a dolman *(left)* and a pelisse *(right)*.

Officers in 1815, in quarters dress.

Officers in 1815, wearing morning dress and frock coat.

Senior officer wearing full dress in 1815.

The Officers of the 2nd Chasseurs à cheval Regiment
Officers at the time the Young Squadrons were created in 1813-1814.
Officers wearing full dress in 1815.
Officers in campaign dress in 1815.

The gardes d'honneur

1813... The Russian and Spanish campaigns had got the better of the Cavalry of the Imperial Guard. Napoleon had to make up its losses by using one of the Empire's last resources: conscription. The Emperor created new units led by experienced officers from other regiments stationed in Germany, Italy or Spain; they made up the Young Guard.

As of January 1813, Napoleon who apparently had not learnt anything from his unfortunate experience with the Gendarmes d'Ordonnance, wanted to create a six-squadron Regiment of Life Guards intended to guard the person of the Emperor and the King of Rome.

In fact, in April, he created four Gardes d'Honneur regiments. They had to be recruited among the sons of the nobility and upper classes, on a volunteer basis.

Indeed, up until then, most of these young men had got out of conscription by paying for a person to replace them. The decree setting up the unit stipulated that the men making up these regiments had to pay for their dress, their equipment and their mounts themselves, but that they would be paid as though they were Chasseurs of the Guard; this last measure was intended to flatter potential volunteers.

But they were few and far between, and faced with such a lack of enthusiasm, the *prefets* were given orders to conscript the men as a matter of course anyway. This of course led to a good number of deserters. Besides, the replacement system still persisted and a good number of young men from the more modest classes were enrolled in the Gardes d'Honneur and dressed and equipped at the expense of wealthier families who thereby managed to get round the vagaries and uncertainties of military life.

The four regiments got themselves more or less well organised and then started campaigning. They were given their baptism of fire at Leipzig and on 30 October, they charged brilliantly at Hanau to disengage the Grenadiers à Cheval of the Guard. Thanks to illness and desertions, the Gardes d'Honneur took part in the French campaign in greatly reduced numbers. On 13 March 1814, they distinguished themselves at Reims during a charge in which they captured a whole Russian battery, though not without heavy casualties. On 30 March at the gates of Paris, the 3rd Gardes d'Honneur charged for the last time...

It was the end. After the abdication at Fontainebleau, the Gardes d'Honneur disappeared: they returned to their families or they were incorporated into the Royal army. Some of them who were aristocrats joined the King's Life Guards.

At Waterloo, 87 Gardes d'Honneur were still present in the cavalry of the Guard

THE UNIFORM

The decree dated 5 April 1813 gives a fill description of the uniform and the equipment of the Gardes d'Honneur. "[...] *The four regiments will be dressed, equipped and armed in the Hussar fashion* [...]*The uniform of the four regiments will be the same: the pelisse will be dark green with white flannel lining and black skin on the border, the edge of the collar, the* boudin *(false pocket) and around the sleeves, together with white cord, braid loops and tresses.*

The background colour of the dolman will be dark green with scarlet facings and collar; there will be also tresses on the collar, false pockets and facings the same colour as the pelisse. The Hungarian-style breeches will be made of red cloth with white braid. The buttons will be white, the belt crimson and white and the shako red."

After a number of incidents, the regiments were eventually formed. But as far as dress, equipment and weapons were concerned, the results were rather catastrophic. Although some Guards wore tailor-made uniforms, most of them wore uniforms cut from poor quality cloth with a wide range of colour shades. The trousers were either too short or too long, or the shakos were too big. In a report dated 13 October 1813, Nansouty wrote: "[...] *These corps are generally badly dressed, badly equipped and badly presented. They also have a lot of bad horses* [...]."

Particular details concerning important points of dress, equipment and weapons are described below.

The shako

This was bulkier than the regulation 1812 model. Made out of strong cardboard or leather, it was covered with red cloth. There was a white thread braid stripe around the upper circumference.

It had a silver brass plate as required by the 1812 regulations, comprising an eagle standing on a base.

The visor was circled with silver metal. The chins trap consisted of a small silver chain sewn onto a strip of red cloth. The cord was plaited with two white thread flounders. In the Gardes d'Honneur, the flounders were worn on the left.

The plume was green; the colour of the tip was the distinctive: red for the 1st Regiment, sky blue for the 2nd, yellow for the 3rd and white for the 4th. There was a pompom the same colour as the squadron at the base of the plume. With the second uniform, the Gardes d'Honneur wore a pompom with a pendant the same colour as the regimental distinctive.

The Forage Cape

This was a common model with a knot; the turban and pennant were made of dark green cloth with scarlet Russian braid; braid made of white thread was sewn to the upper edge of the turban. The inside of the headpiece was made of natural coloured heavy cloth.

The cavalry hat

The hat was the bicorn usually worn by the cavalry. It had a cockade held in place by a white wool cord fastened with a semi-spherical button made of silver metal. The officers had a hat with braid and silver tresses.

The dolman

This item was made of dark green cloth[1] "lined with undyed coloured canvas, and waist-high red hide" [2]. The collar and the facings were scarlet. There were eighteen rows of white tresses on the front. The false pockets, the collar braid and that on the facings were made of white tresses.

The buttons, like with the officers – *"noblesse oblige"* – were semi-spherical and made of silver metal. There were 91 buttons sewn onto the dolman: 72 medium-sized ones for the two rows on each side, 18 large ones for the middle row and a medium one for the left-hand shoulder flap.

The pelisse,

This item of clothing was made of dark green cloth like the dolman; the lining was made of white flannel. The

1. In Elbeuf or Berry cloth according Christian Blondieau.
2. « Les gardes d'honneur » by Christian Blondieau, in *Uniformes* n° 47.

pelisse was edged with black fur on the collar, the front and the end of the sleeves. Eighteen white tresses like on the dolman carried five rows of 18 buttons.

The Waistcoat

This was made of scarlet cloth and was sleeveless. The collar, the waist and the false pockets were all edged with white braid. This item had 18 rows of white tresses with five series of medium-sized buttons. This was never worn in full dress.

The Coat

This important item of clothing was also made of green cloth with sleeves, with a straight collar fastened by two little flaps.

The Little Uniform

On 16 June 1813, the Gardes d'Honneur received a little uniform made up of a tail coat made of green cloth with scarlet facings. The piping on the lapels was the same. The aiglets were white. The green cloth breeches had white braid motifs; the waistcoat was scarlet with white tresses.

The Sash-Belt

This was the Hussar model. This belt was 8 ft 6 in (2.60 m) long, and made up of 44 little crimson cords with twenty loops. It was worn outside the dolman and had to go around the waist three times. Some Guards, who were not *"au fait"* with the subtleties of "Hungarian fashion", wore it over the pelisse.

The Stable Jacket

Although the regulations described it as being made of dark green knitwear, the stable jacket finally supplied was made of dark green Elbeuf or de Berry cloth, like the dolman or the pelisse. The collar, the shoulder flaps and the facings were the same colour. The jacket was fastened with fifteen medium-sized buttons and was worn with canvas or white twill trousers.

The Breeches

These were naturally Hungarian. They were made of the same cloth as the dolman but this time it was scarlet. A white tress was sewn along the seam. It was garnished with pointed motifs on the thigh fronts.

The Riding Breeches

While the troops were marching or campaigning, the red breeches were replaced by green cloth breeches. This item buttoned from top to bottom with 18 large buttons sewn as usual on a thick scarlet cloth stripe.

These trousers had a large fly and had a 1 in (25 mm) wide foot strap. Calfskin lining was sewn from top to bottom to reinforce the inside of the legs. In the closing months of the Empire this item was made of grey cloth.

The Boots

These were the light cavalry models; they had gussets and were made up of two pieces of assembled black leather. Some of the boots were given white braid with a woollen tassel the same colour as the upper edge; others had only a black leather knot sewn onto the front, cut out in the shape of a heart.

Some Guards seem to have been given ones without any decoration at all. A horseshoe held on with five screws protected the heel. The spurs were made of copper and were either screwed or nailed on.

IMPERIAL GUARD OR NOT IMPERIAL GUARD

Were the Gardes d'Honneur really part of the Imperial Guard?

It is true that Article 6 of the decree dated 5 April 1813 stipulated that: "[...] *they would have the pay of the Chasseurs of the Guard* [...]."

Moreover they wore the same straight embroidery and aiglet on their uniforms as the Guard. These elements would seem to indicate that they belonged to the Guard.

But on April 25, the Minister Director of the War administration announced that *"under the present system of financing, the regiments of the Gardes d'Honneur will be assimilated to the Line Corps"*.

Although the Emperor wanted them to serve him, like at the Battle of Leipzig, and clearly intended to incorporate them into the Imperial Guard, he never actually decided to make it official once and for all.

The Cartridge Case and its Strap

This was the model used by the Hussars. The cartridge case consisted of a wooden coffer, covered with blackened calfskin. The flap was fastened by a buckle and tongue sewn under the coffer.[3]

The cartridge case belt, sometimes called a baldric, was made of white buffalo hide, stopped by two rows of stitching on the case's rings. The loops and the buckles were made of copper.

The Musketoon Belt

This was also made of white buffalo hide, with a two-tongued square buckle. The rings and the ornaments were made of copper. The musketoon belt had a little strap made of shrunk buffalo hide.

The Belt

This was the light cavalry model. It was made of white buffalo hide and could be adjusted using a tongue buckle on the right side[4]. It was fastened by a brass buckle, forming two square tenons on the front. The belt was fitted with a bayonet holder holding a black leather scabbard.

The Sabretache

This was made from black, varnished leather and had a crowned eagle above the regimental number.

The Weapons

The Gardes d'Honneur were in theory armed with an An-XI-model light cavalry sabre and a cavalry musketoon and a pair of An-XIII-model pistols.

The Harnesses

These were the models issued to all light cavalry units. The wooden saddle had a tree with iron-tipped forks with wooden screws. A pair of wooden iron-ringed holsters was covered in pelt. The straps, stirrup leather, cruppers, belts and other barrel holders were made of Hungarian leather.

The buckles were so-called "roll-buckles". The schabrack, like the stirrups, was Hussar-style. It was made from festooned sheepskin with dark green cloth. The bridle headstall, the reins, and the plaited whip were all Hussar-style.

The buckles were tin-plated. The bridle bit had curb chains; the net was made of black leather, like the so-called "parade" halter with the tether.

3. « Les gardes d'honneur » by Christian Blondieau, in *Uniformes* n° 47.
4. Ibid.

A white wool hussar-style blanket, a black leather stable headstall, a head bag (for eating) and two bags for the horseshoes completed the harnessing.

The Portmanteau

This was made of green cloth with white thread braid round both ends, surrounding the regimental number cut out of white cloth.

THE TRUMPETERS

In theory, the trumpeters in the four regiments of the Gardes d'Honneur had to wear Imperial Livery, defined in the 1812 Regulations: dolman and dark green pelisse whose sleeves were decorated with seven yellow and green stripes. In reality, other uniforms were also worn, each regiment wanting to distinguish itself from the others.

The plumes were the opposite colours of those of the troopers. The regiments wanted to distinguish themselves very quickly from the others by using several uniform combinations.

In the 1st Regiment

The trumpeter wore a white colback with a scarlet pennant, surmounted by a sky blue plume, one third of which was scarlet. A silver chinstrap made up the headdress.

The pelisse was made of scarlet cloth with white tresses, gold buttons, gold braid on the facings. The breeches were made of chamois skin and were stuffed into the light cavalry boots. The sabretache was covered with scarlet cloth edged with gold braid. A yellow metal eagle surmounted the regimental number cut out from the same metal *(see page 41)*.

Another trumpeter is shown wearing the red trooper's shako with a silver metal plate, a one third scarlet dark green plume, and a white cord. The dolman was sky blue with white tresses, gold buttons, scarlet gold braided collar and facings. As for the pelisse, it was made of scarlet cloth edged with black fur, decorated with white tresses. The buttons and the stripes were gold. The breeches were scarlet and its motifs were made of white and sky blue tress.

The sabretache was made of black leather with an eagle and silver number *(see page 41)*. The trumpet cord was apparently blue.

In the Second Regiment

The shako was probably that of the troopers covered with a black, waxed cloth cover when they wore campaigning dress. The pompom was blue.

The dolman was also sky blue with white tresses, white buttons, white braided scarlet collar and facings.

The riding breeches were red with a white seam stripe with silver buttons. The black-tinted sheepskin schabrack had green cloth wolf's teeth festoons; the portmanteau was made of green cloth with white braid. The trumpet cord was green *(see page 48)*.

According to certain pictorial sources a trumpeter can be seen wearing a black colback with a scarlet pennant and a green plume whose the upper third is sky blue. The dolman was once again sky blue with white tresses, white buttons, white braided scarlet collar and facings. The pelisse was like the dolman: sky blue with white buttons, braid and tresses.

The Hungarian-style breeches were red with white braid, aces and distinctives. It was red with a blue seam stripe and silver buttons.

The black-tinted sheepskin schabrack had wolf's teeth festoons made of green cloth; the portmanteau was also made of green cloth with white braid. The trumpet cord was red this time *(see page 48)*.

In the 3rd Regiment

Still according to contemporary sources, the trumpeters apparently wore a trooper's shako with a yellow pennant and pompom. The dolman was scarlet and the blue cloth pelisse had white tresses and buttons the same colour.

The riding breeches were made of green cloth with scarlet piping. The black- tinted sheepskin schabrack had green cloth wolf's teeth festoons; the portmanteau was made of green cloth with white braid. The trumpet cord was red *(see page 48)*.

In the 4th Regiment

The picture of the non-regulation uniform of a trumpeter from the 4th Regiment comes from a canvas showing Napoleon at the Battle of Leipzig with an escort from this regiment

The shako was red with a gold metal plate and chinstrap. The dolman was red with white tresses; the riding breeches were red with a yellow or gold seam stripe. The schabrack was apparently made of red cloth, edged with yellow or gold braid *(see pages 56 and 54)*.

A band for the Gardes d'Honneur is mentioned in the little Strasbourg collection of cardboard soldiers. Did it really exist? To which regiment should it be attributed? Nothing enables us to assert anything nowadays with any certainty.

The Grooms

The wealthier guards had asked to be allowed to be accompanied by a servant. This privilege, granted by decree, must have caused a lot of resentment among the men of the Old Guard: "[...] *For every two mounted Gardes d'Honneur, a groom will be appointed, under the name of "tartar"* [...] *Each tartar will look after the horses of the two Gardes d'Honneur as well as his own* [...]."

And yes, you have read correctly: the decree makes no mention of officers specifically, so it also concerns the simple troopers.

The NCOs and the officers

The NCOs' shako cord, the dolman, pelisse and waistcoat tresses should have been made of silver mixed with green, but the pictures show us that the regulations were not strictly respected. The officers wore the same uniform as the troopers, but it was cut from finer cloth. The shako stripes and the flounder cords were silver. They sometimes wore a colback with a scarlet flame piped with silver and, at the end of the Empire, the shako-rouleau. The trimmings of the dolman, the pelisse, the waistcoat and the breeches were silver, and often gold among the senior officers.

The usually sumptuous equipment was made of black, red or green leather and could have fancy braiding. The sabretaches were covered in cloth garnished with braid and the ornaments were embroidered in silver and sometimes in gold.

The Troopers in the 1st Gardes d'Honneur Regiment

Garde d'Honneur in the 1st Regiment wearing full dress, according to the Musee de l'Armee Collections.

Garde d'Honneur from the 1st Regiment wearing exercise dress, according to a water- colour by Lucien Rousselot.

Garde d'Honneur from the 1st Regiment wearing full dress, according to a drawing of Dutch origin.

Garde d'Honneur from the 1st Regiment wearing full dress, according to Martinet's engravings.

1st Regiment Sabretache.

The Troopers in the 1st Gardes d'Honneur Regiment.

Garde d'Honneur in the 1st Regiment wearing full dress according to Martinet's engravings, but they could be from after the Hundred Days.

Town dress according to a drawing by L. Rousselot. It seems that this uniform was rarely worn.

Garde d'Honneur in the 1st Regiment wearing a pelisse. A period anecdote recounts that some guards, unaccustomed to wearing Hussar dress, tied their scarves over the pelisse.

The Trumpeters in the 1st Gardes d'Honneur Regiment

Trumpeter, according to a uniform as described by Commandant Bucquoy.

Trumpeter, according to a uniform as described by H. Boisselier.

Trumpeter, according to a uniform described by contemporary sources. Note the braid on the breeches, which is white mixed with sky blue, and the buttons which were gold.

The Troopers in the 1st Gardes d'Honneur Regiment

A Garde wearing campaign dress.

Groom assigned to the Gardes d'Honneur, something which must have made a lot of the men of the Old Guard envious, which was the reason the groom had to look after two troopers from among the wealthier men.

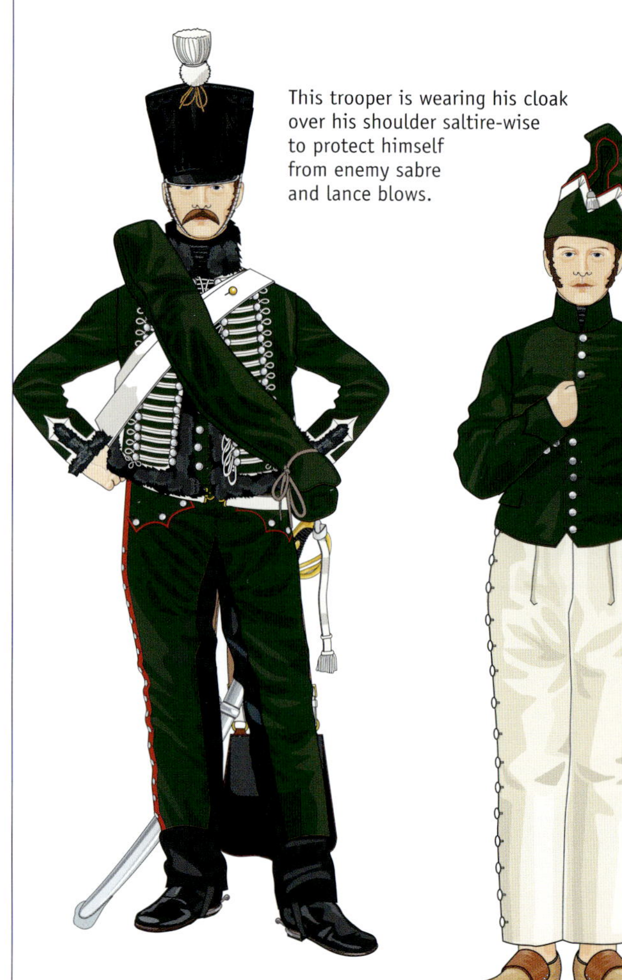

This trooper is wearing his cloak over his shoulder saltire-wise to protect himself from enemy sabre and lance blows.

A Garde wearing stable dress.

General Charles-Joseph Randon de Malboissière de Pully

Born on 18 December 1751, he started his military career on 22 April 1768 as a volunteer in the Bercheny Hussars; on the following 2 December, he went over to the 1st Company of Musketeers of the Kings Household with the rank of lieutenant. On 11 April 1770, he was a captain in la Rochefoucauld's Dragoons. First a squadron commander in May 1788, then a lieutenant-colonel in the Royal-Cravates on 17 May 1789, he became a colonel on 5 February 1792 and was then appointed brigadier-general on 19 September of the same year. Promoted to major-general on 8 March 1793, he was however relieved of his command on 1 August 1793.

He was reinstated in 1794 and an order from the Directoire in 1795 appointed him Inspector-General of Cavalry. He was one of the first to join General Bonaparte on 18 Brumaire.

During the Empire he was given the task of inspecting the cavalry stationed in Italy. On 5 January 1812, he was called to Versailles to organise the 1st Regiment of the Gardes d'Honneur; Napoleon appointed him their colonel on 8 April 1813. Napoleon also awarded him the title of Count of the Empire the same year.

When the Emperor abdicated the first time, General Pully sent his submission to Louis XVIII. In 1814 and 1815, he held the post of Inspector-General of Cavalry and retired in 1815. He welcomed the July 1830 Revolution with as much enthusiasm as that of 1789. He died in Paris on 20 April 1832.

The General Pully

Troopers in the 1st Regiment

Officer wearing full dress. Note the upper black velvet stripe on the shako enhanced by a series of rings.

Trumpeter, according to a uniform described by contemporary sources. Note the buttons which are gold and the sabretache plate made of brass.

Officer in campaign dress.

Officer wearing social dress according to Lucien Rousselot.

Officer wearing a frock coat.

Standard-Bearer

Garde d'Honneur in the Second Regiment. This rear view enables the way the equipment was placed to be seen.

The Gardes d'Honneur levied in 1813 in the *Bouche de la Meuse*, a new French department since 1811, had to join the Second Regiment which was being formed. This emblem, made by the prefet's wife, was issued to them when they left. When they reached Metz however, General Lepic, the colonel commanding the regiment, insisted on the pennant being destroyed because it was not a regulation one. Nonetheless an identical example has been preserved in the Amsterdam Museum, which suggests that in the end the pennant escaped destruction, or that a second model was made as a souvenir of their campaigning when the Dutch Guards returned home.

Garde d'Honneur from the 2nf Regiment wearing full dress.

The Trumpeters from the 2nd Regiment

Trumpeter in campaign dress, according to an aquarelle by Lucien Rousselot.

Trumpeter wearing full dress, according to a drawing by J. Girbal for Dr Hourtoulle's collection of plates.

Trumpeter wearing full dress, according to the 1812 Regulations.

Trumpeter in campaign dress, according to an aquarelle by H. Boisselier.

The 2nd Regiment of Gardes d'Honneur

Garde wearing campaign dress. Note he is wearing a full-dress plume on his shako protected by a waxed cloth cover.

Marechal des logis wearing full dress. The tresses were silver when they ought to have been a mix of green and silver.

Officer in campaign dress, wearing the pelisse over his shoulder.

Officer in campaign dress, wearing the pelisse.

The 3rd Regiment of Gardes d'Honneur

Uniform worn by the second colonel this could be Colonel Vincent, with the rank of brigadier-general.

Officer wearing frock coat.

Trumpeter wearing Imperial livery, according to the 1812 regulations.

Trumpeter, according to a drawing by J. Girbal for Dr Hourtoulle's collection.

Trumpeter, according to a description appearing in the magazine *Uniformes* n°47.

Garde in campaign dress.

Trooper wearing full dress according to an engraving by A. Martinet.

Garde during the Campaign for France. Note the 3rd Regiment's particular positioning of the shako cords.

Uniform worn by the Count of Belmont-Brançion, colonel-major in the 3rd Regiment. He was killed during the Campaign for France at the Battle of Reims, on 13 March 1814.

Raymond Gaspard de Bonardi, Count of Saint-Sulpice, was born on 23 October 1761 in Paris. He was appointed sous-lieutenant in the 13th Dragoon Regiment on 29 September 1777, a few months after he started his military career.

A captain in the Dragoons of Monsieur, the future Louis XVIII, in 1781, he was promoted to colonel of the 12th Dragoons Regiment on 26 October 1792.

His aristocratic origins caused him some trouble during the Revolutionary Wars, but did not prevent him from being promoted to brigadier-general on 24 March 1803, then to Commander of the Legion d'Honneur on 14 June 1804. He took part in the Prussian and Polish campaigns, commanding the 2nd Cuirassier Brigade, and fought at Jena then Eylau on 8 February 1807, where a bullet broke both his wrists. Promoted to Major General on 14 February 1807, he was made a Count of the Empire in 1808. In 1809 he joined the Dragoons of the Imperial Guard then, in 1813, he was Governor of the Chateau of Fontainebleau. He commanded the 4th Regiment of Gardes d'Honneur in Saxony and at Lyon in 1814.

He was promoted to Grand Officier of the Legion d'Honneur and was awarded the Croix de Chevalier of Saint-Louis by Louis XVIII. He was admitted to the office of the paymaster then retired in 1815. He died in Paris on 20 June 1835.

A Garde in campaign dress note that the Gardes often wore the plume a nd the shako as for full dress.

A Garde wearing a coat.

A Garde wearing full dress.

Raymond Gaspard de Bonardi, Count of Saint-Sulpice, wearing the full-dress uniform of the colonel commanding the 4th Gardes d'Honneur Regiment.

The NCOs in the 4th Gardes d'Honneur Regiment

Marechal des Logis wearing full dress, after the Musee de l'Emperi's collections.

Brigadier wearing full dress. Note the string of rings along the upper stripe of the shako.

Marechal des logis chef wearing town dress. The aiglet belongs to the Musee de l' Armee's collection.

A Garde wearing campaign dress 1813-1814.

The Trumpeters from the 4th Gardes d'Honneur Regiment

Trumpeter from the 4th Gardes d'honneur Regiment wearing a non-regulation campaign dress.

Trumpeter from the 4th Gardes d'honneur Regiment wearing a a non-regulation full dress.

Trumpeter from the 4th Gardes d'honneur Regiment campaign dress, according to the regulations.

The Trumpeters from the 4th Gardes d'Honneur Regiment

Campaign dress 1813-1814. Note the gold and silver on the tresses.

Trumpeter wearing full dress according to Knötel. It was the same dress as the 2nd Regiment's, but the plume was the colour of the 4th Regiment.

The Gardes d'Honneur uniform

Trooper's shako for the four Garde d'Honneur regiments. Some descriptions say that the Garde d'Honneur shako was bigger than the other corps' hat. Other sources show shakos which were more flared around the top; some resembled those worn by the Rhine Confederation troops.
The shako was worn to the end under the First Restoration, as its attributes indicate.

Shirt.

Waistcoat.

Pelisse.

Forage cap

Stable waistcoat.

Buttons.

Dolman.

Braces.

Sash belt.

Breeches.

Riding breeches.

Chasseur-style coat.

Weapons and equipment

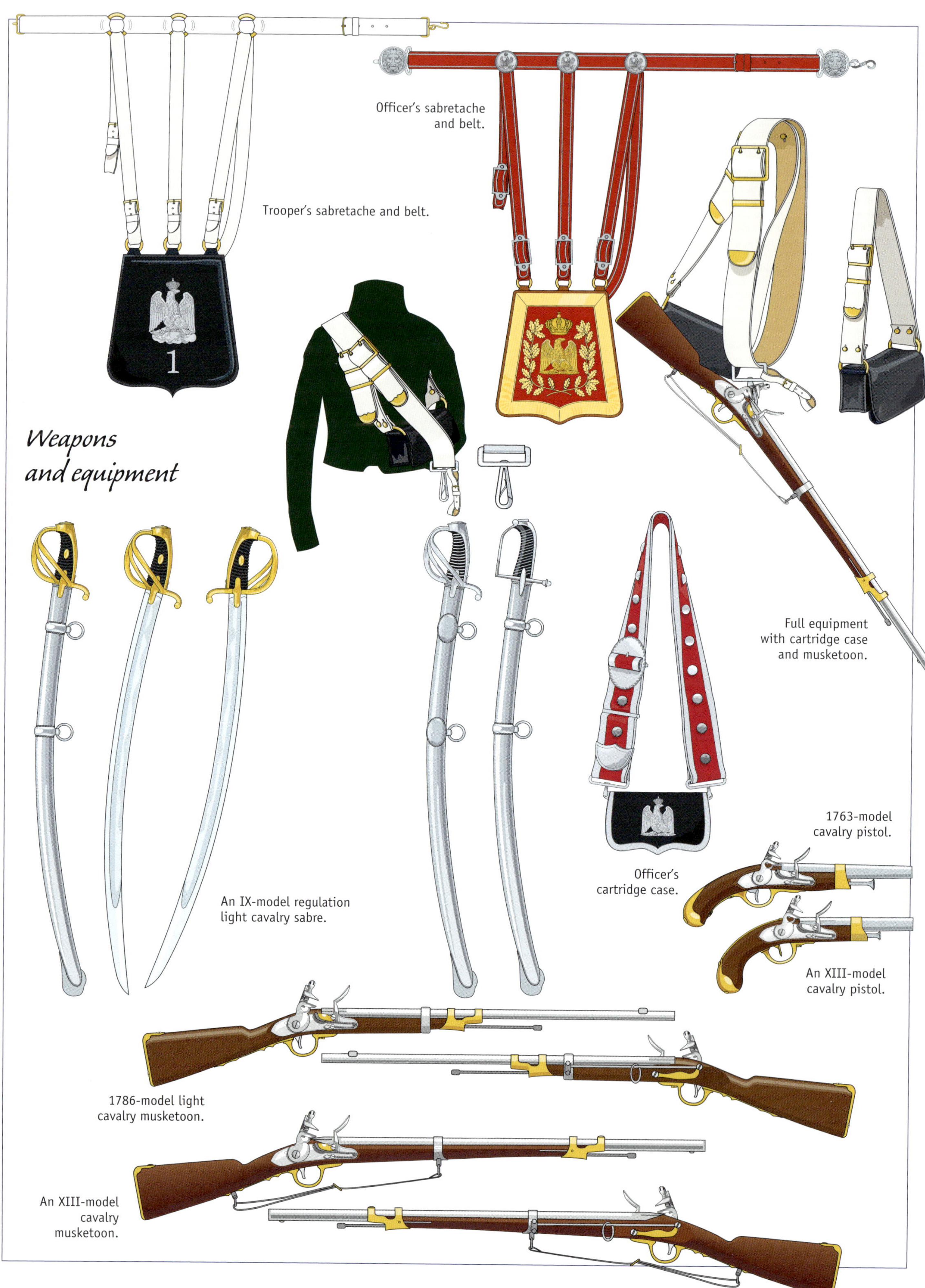

Portmanteau
(open)
Hungarian-style
bridle.
Hungarian-style light cavalry
saddle made up of a wooden tree
and a leather seat. It rested
on a blanket and was held
in place by an under-belly strap.
The crupper went under the horse's
tail and was fastened to
the saddle by means of a little
buckle. At the front, the pistol holsters
were attached to the tree with a strap
and the barrel boot was fastened to the right-hand holster.
Schabrack,
from
the off-side.
Schabrack,
from the on-side.
Trumpeter's Schabrack.
Officer's and senior
officer's saddlecloth.
Colonel-major's
saddlecloth.
Officer's parade
saddlecloth.

The Eclaireurs of the Guard

The idea of creating the Eclaireur regiments which, as a result, were "light" cavalry, came no doubt from the impression the Cossacks made, armed as they were, with lances during the Russian Campaign. Napoleon even declared: *"I've always wanted some; our cavalry is too heavy against the Cossacks."*

On 4 and 9 December 1813, two decrees gave the new composition of the Cavalry of the Guard and ordered three Eclaireur (Scout) regiments to be created with four 250-man squadrons each.

Still intent on creating units capable of countering the Cossacks, the Emperor had the Eclaireurs armed with lances. Each regiment was assigned to a corps of the Guard: the 1st Eclaireurs to the Grenadiers à cheval, the 2nd to the Dragoons, the 3rd to the 1 Chevau-Legers Lancers. Half of the regiments were expected to be ready by 1 January 1814, the rest by 30 January.

Organising the 1st Eclaireurs Regiment fell to Colonel Testot-Ferry. The men were raised from the 1st, 3rd and 4th Gardes d'Honneur.

The Second Regiment would not provide any men because it was blockaded in Mainz. The first two squadrons, in the Old Guard, were therefore made up of troopers from the Guard and the Line.

The other two squadrons, in the Young Guard, were raised with conscripts and troopers from the Line. All the officers and NCOs came from the Guard[1].

The Eclaireurs joined the army by detachments to swell the ranks of the cavalry and fought until the capitulation of Paris.

They were dismissed when Napoleon abdicated the first time.

The Eclaireurs had five or six-year-old horses, measuring from 4 feet 2 inches to 4 feet 3 inches at the withers (1.353 to 1.380 m).

THE IMPERIAL DECREE DATED 9 DECEMBER 1813

Chapter one: the Organisation of the Cavalry of the Guard

[...]

- Article one

Three regiments of Eclaireurs à cheval have been created in our Guard. Each regiment will consist of four squadrons; each squadron will comprise 250 men.

- Article 2

The 1st Regiment of Eclaireurs will be attached to the Grenadiers à cheval; it will be under the orders of the Colonel of the Grenadiers à Cheval and administered by the arm's board. The Second Regiment will be attached to the Dragoons, commanded by the Colonel of the Dragoons and administered by the Dragoons' board. Finally the 3rd Regiment will be attached to the 1st Regiment of Lancers commanded and administered by this regiment.

- Article 3

The Grenadiers à Cheval, Dragoons, Chasseurs and 2nd Lancers regiments will all keep their present organisation; the 1st Lancer Regiment will be organised according to Table N° 1, attached to the present decree.

Chapter Two
Recruitment

- Article 4

200 men will be chosen from among the Gardes d'Honneur regiments to make up the cavalry regiments of our Guard. Thirty men are going to be used to complete the Grenadiers à Cheval regiment; they must be 5 feet 5 inches tall. 30 men are intended for the Dragoons and must be 5 feet 4 inches tall. 140 men are intended for the 2nd Lancer Regiment and will be at least 5 feet 1 inch tall. The choice of these 200 men will be made without delay from each of the Gardes d'Honneur regiments. The designated men will be sent to Paris dismounted. They will be fitted out and remounted in their new regiments.

- Article 5

Each of the four Gardes d'Honneur regiments will supply 250 men to make up the 1st Eclaireurs Regiment; the designated men will go to Paris dismounted but fitted out and armed. The Second Regiment of Eclaireurs will be recruited by a levy of 1,000 men from the Empire. Our Minister of Finance will prepare a report on the manner in which this levy will be carried out.

The 3rd Regiment of Eclaireurs will be recruited with the men from the 1st Regiment of Lancers exceeding the quota set out by the new organisation and by 800 men "who will be chosen at Sedan from among the Poles of goodwill who have served France for a long time.

These men will be directed to Givet to be fitted out and remounted.

Chapter 3
Remounts

- Article 6

The Colonels in the cavalry regiments of the Guard will organise the purchase of horses: 300 for the Grenadiers à cheval; 450 for the Dragoons; 700 for the chasseurs; 210 for the Lancers; in all a total of 1,650 horses.

All these horses must be at least six years old. Half will be ready for 10 January and the other half for the 30th of the same month. Harnessing will be supplied immediately so that on 15 February all the corps will be ready and mounted.

- Article 7

The horses in the three Eclaireurs regiments will be ready at the same time.

The Colonels of the Grenadiers, the Dragoons, the 1st Lancers will work together to set up the purchase of 3,000 horses which are at least six years old and 3 feet 4 inches high; any horse which is 5 *[Illegible]* will be withdrawn from the Eclaireurs and given to the Lancers. *[Illegible]* is granted to the Eclaireurs' horses.

Chapter 4
Dress - Pay

- Article 8

The 1st Regiment of Eclaireurs will wear the Gardes d'Honneurs' uniform, the Second Regiment that of the Chasseurs of the Line and the 3rd that of the Polish Lancers of the Line.

- Article 9

The officers, NCOs and Eclaireurs in the 1st Regiment will have the same rank as the Old Guard. They will be paid like the 1st Chasseurs Regiment. They will not have the right to the remount and reshoeing sums, for the first time and for the first mount.

The 2nd and 3rd Eclaireurs officers will have the same rank and pay as the Guard; the NCOs and Eclaireurs in these two regiments will have the same rank as in the Line and will be considered as corresponding to the 2nd Chasseur à Cheval Regiment of the Guard [...]."

1. According to Commandant Bucquoy (in « le Passepoil », 1923) the 1st and 2nd Squadrons were the Old Guard, whereas the 3rd and 4th were Young Guard. The 2nd and 3rd Regiments were only Young Guard, except for their officers.

The Troopers in the 1st Eclaireur Regiment

Brigadier wearing full dress, after a plate from "le Plumet" by Rigo.

Trooper wearing full dress after an aquarelle by Lucien Rousselot, seen from the on-side and the off-side.

Trooper wearing full dress in 1813.

The 1st Eclaireurs Regiment

The 1st Regiment was set up by Colonel Testot-Ferry and sometimes called the "Eclaireurs-Grenadiers Regiment". The majority of the officers came from the Old Guard cavalry regiments.

The four Gardes d'Honneur regiments furnished 250 men each. The first roll of the corps (Old Guard) showed 506 roll numbers (for 501 men), the second roll (Young Guard) 608.

The 1st Regiment was organised at the Ecole Militaire in Paris and grew rapidly from four to six squadrons "by adding two squadrons of Gardes d'Honneur, made up of young people from good families."

At the end of the month of January, the regiment joined the main part of the army which was fighting on French soil. Barely two months later, there were only 200 troopers left. They distinguished themselves at Craonne and Arcis-sur-Aube.

After the abdication the regiment was dismissed on 12 May 1814.

Uniform of the 1st Eclaireurs Regiment

The typical uniform of the Eclaireurs of the Young Guard companies was an habit-veste without lapels; it was green enhanced with scarlet and was mentioned in particular in the tailoring and distribution returns.

It was almost the same as the à la Kinski habit-veste which the Chasseurs à Cheval had adopted in around 1808-1809 and, with its scarlet-coloured collar and facings, it greatly resembled that of the 1st Chasseurs.

The shako

This was black and cylindrical and according to contemporary pictures seems to have been shorter than the Hussars' shako-rouleau.

A black velvet stripe with a string of scarlet rings surrounded its upper circumference. The front was decorated with a white metal eagle under a tricolour cockade. The chin strap, held in place by two lion's head clasps, consisted of a small chain mounted on a leather strip. The visor had a white metal edge. In full dress, a scarlet plume with a black base surmounted the shako. This headdress was common to both the Old ad the Young Guard Squadrons.

The coat

The Old Guard squadrons wore a dark green pelisse ornamented with white tresses and round white metal buttons. Dolmans and Hungarian breeches were scarcely used. The Young Guard squadrons wore a dark green short-tailed coat (habit-veste), fastened down the front with 9 round white metal buttons. The collar, facings, turnbacks and edges of the shoulder flaps were scarlet.

The trousers

These were very full, made of grey cloth and decorated with a scarlet stripe down the leg; they fastened at the bottom of the leg with eight buttons. There was blackened calfskin lining between the legs ending with a small band on each leg. This was the model used by most of the cavalry corps in the Guard campaigning at the end of the Empire.

The main equipment

For all the squadrons, this comprised a cartridge case, its shoulder strap and a musketoon holder strap, like those used by the light cavalry of the Line. The strapping was not stitched.

In theory the Old Guard squadrons wore a belt with sabretache straps, but apparently not all the troopers received this. The Young Guard Squadrons were equipped with the belt used by the Chasseurs à Cheval of the Line.

Weapons

The Lancer ranks were armed with an 1812-model lance and an An-XIII model pistol hanging from the musketoon holder strap. Carabineer ranks were armed with the An-XIII musketoon. Everybody was issued with an An-XI-model light cavalry sabre. *"Half the Eclaireurs were armed with lances with crimson and white pennants, the other half with musketoons. All had two pistols and a curved sabre with a metal scabbard."*

Saddlery

The various sources consulted reveal that two types of saddle were used: the classic Hungarian-style saddle covered with a white or scarlet striped schabrack; and lighter Hungarian leather saddle with panels just placed on a grey blanket. Given the situation, the latter was most probably used because of concern over simplification and cost reduction.

For the same reason the head harnessing was also simplified, but it was not in general use throughout the regiment.

THE ECLAIREURS IN ACTION

Arriving as they did too late in the Napoleonic epic to be able to participate in a lot of glorious deeds, the Eclaireurs only took part in one campaign, the Campaign for France, in 1814.

The first squadrons were launched into combat at Brienne on 29 January.

The next day, on 30 January, they charged bravely at la Rothière, shouting: *"Long live the Emperor!"*

On 7 February, the Eclaireur Brigade was disbanded and the regiments went back to the ones they depended on. Thus, at Champaubert, a squadron from the 3rd Regiment was engaged and distinguished itself on the battlefield.

At Montmirail, the squadrons from the 1st and 2nd Eclaireur Regiments fought alongside the Dragoons of the Guard and broke through eight Russian battalions.

On 5 March it was the 3rd Eclaireurs once again which distinguished themselves at the Battle of Berry-au-Bac.

At Craonne, the regiments suffered their heaviest losses. They were led in terrible charges by Testot-Ferry who was awarded the title of Baron of the Empire by Napoleon.

On 15 March, under the command of General Sebastiani – now the commander-in-chief of the Cavalry of the Guard – the 2nd and 3rd Eclaireur Regiments in the Exelmans Division (the 2nd Division of the Cavalry of the Guard) and the 1st Eclaireur Regiment of the 3rd Division, commanded by General Letort, were still present.

The Eclaireurs were committed at Reims, then at Arcis-sur-Aube. It was here, during this battle, that Testot-Ferry and his Eclaireurs saved Napoleon from capture.

The baron was wounded and taken prisoner that day.

The Eclaireurs charged one last time at Saint-Dizier and were once again present at the Battle of Paris, during the capital's brief siege. During this campaign the Eclaireurs' losses were up to the level of their commitment.

The 1st Regiment lost 13 officers and 50 Eclaireurs, the 2nd 17 officers and 100 Eclaireurs; the 3rd Regiment probably suffered the same sort of losses as those in the Second Regiment.

The Troopers in the 1st Eclaireur Regiment

Trooper wearing full dress in 1813.

Trooper wearing a coat in 1813.

Brigadier wearing full dress after a plate in "le Plumet". In April 1814, the Regiment had not yet been disbanded, but the brigadier did hasten to show his Bourbon sympathies.

Trooper, according to Lienhart & Humbert.

Troopers from old and Young guards squadrons

Brigadier from an Old Guard Squadron wearing Campaign dress.

Trooper from a Young Guard Squadron wearing coat and ridding breeches.

Trooper from an Old Guard Squadron wearing Campaign dress.

Trooper, mounted, from a Young Guard Squadron wearing coat and ridding breeches.

The Trumpeters

Trumpeter in campaign dress, according to a drawing by Lucien Rousselot.

Trumpeter in full dress.

Trumpeter in full dress, according to a drawing by H. Boisselier.

Brigadier-trumpeter in full dress, according to the book by Raoul and Jean Brunon devoted to the Eclaireurs.

The Young Guard Squadron

Eclaireur from the Young Guard squadron with an 1812 coat.

Eclaireur from the Young Guard squadron wearing full dress.

Eclaireur from the Young Guard squadron with an 1812 coat.

Adjudant NCO in the Eclaireurs of the Young Guard. The adjudant was distinguishable by the three stripes above his cuffs.

The Eclaireurs of the 1st Regiment

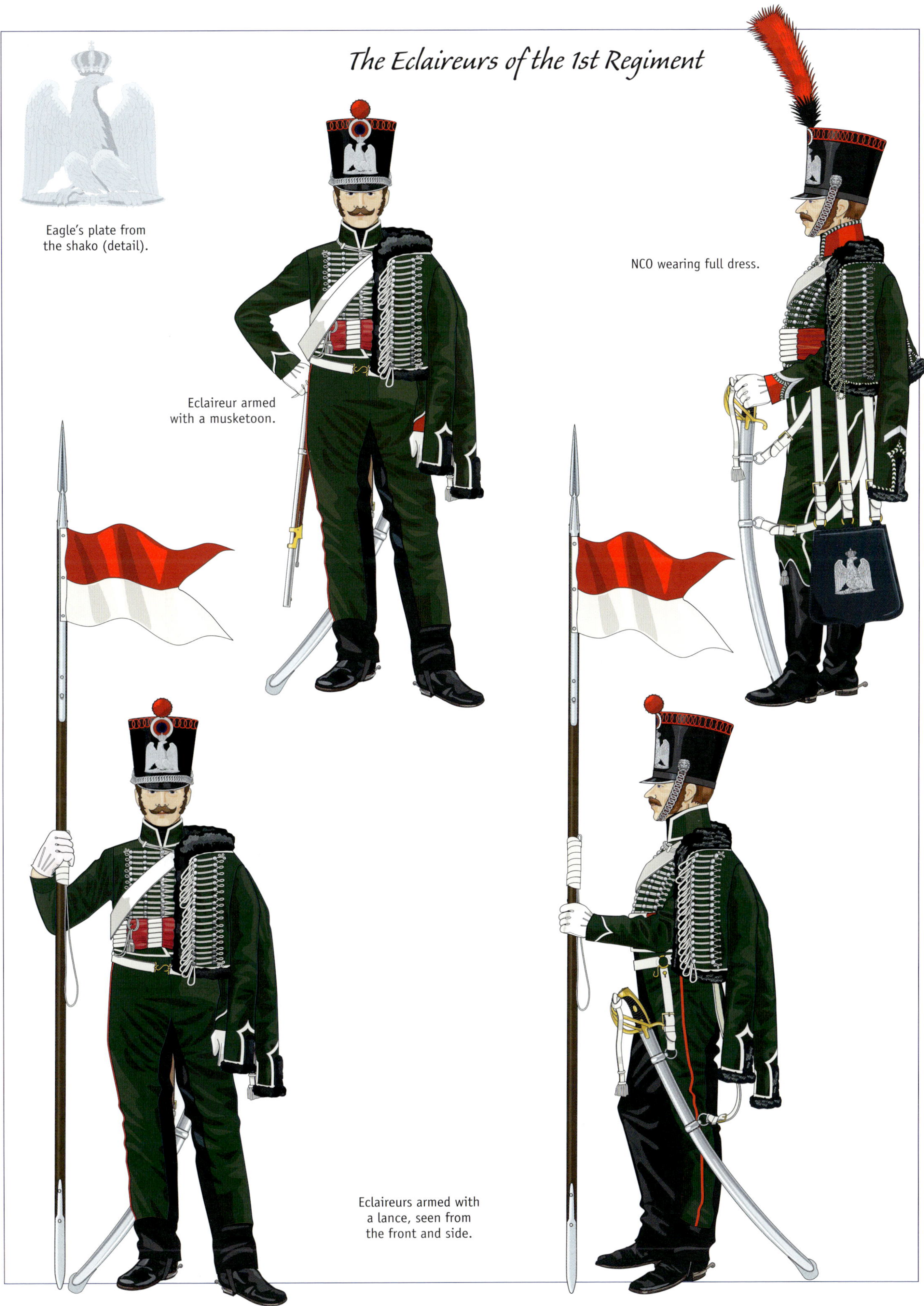

Eagle's plate from the shako (detail).

Eclaireur armed with a musketoon.

NCO wearing full dress.

Eclaireurs armed with a lance, seen from the front and side.

The Eclaireurs in the 1st and 2nd ranks

Eclaireur from the 1st Regiment from the first rank, dismounted, wearing campaign dress.

Eclaireur from the 1st Regiment from the second rank, wearing campaign dress.

Eclaireur from the 1st Regiment from the first rank, mounted, wearing campaign dress.

Eclaireur from the 1st Regiment from the second rank, mounted, wearing campaign dress.

The 1st Eclaireur Regiment officers

Uniform worn by Colonel-Major Testot-Ferry, after a drawing by P. Begnini. Note that the only uniform item to come down to us is the dolman, preserved in the Musee de l'Emperi.

Uniform worn by Colonel-Major Testot-Ferry, after a drawing by P. Begnini. Note that the only uniform item to come down to us is the dolman, preserved in the Musee de l'Emperi.

Officers wearing town dress.
The one on the left is wearing a shako-rouleau, according to a drawing by H. Boisselier.

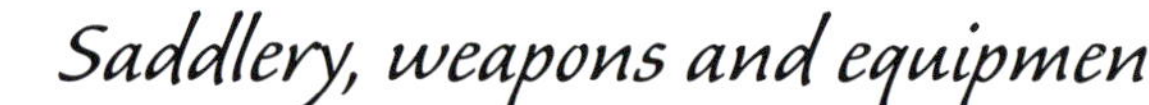

Saddlery, weapons and equipment

Portmanteau.

Type of simplified saddle used by the Eclaireurs.

Type of simplified saddle used by the Eclaireurs it had no holsters as the pistols were carried on a bandoleer. The coat was fastened over the front of the saddle and the portmanteau on the saddle cantle.

Cartridge case and musketoon strap.

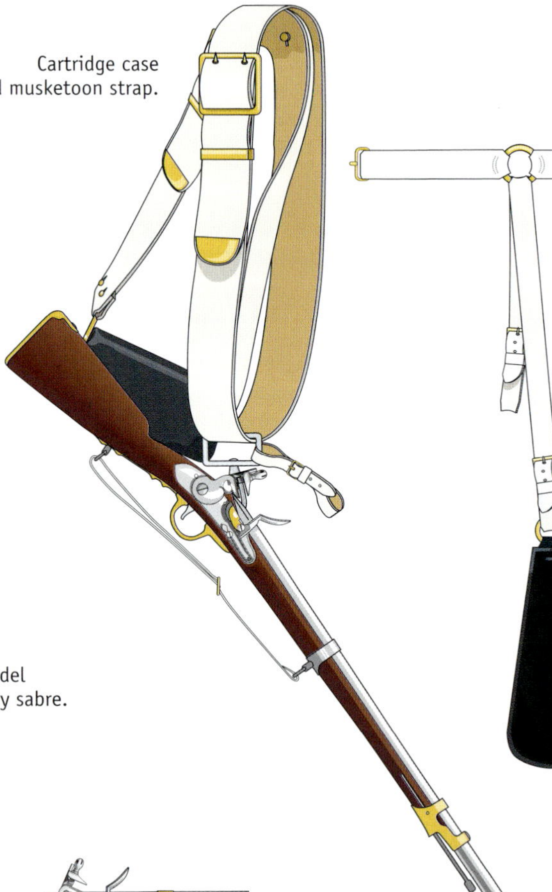

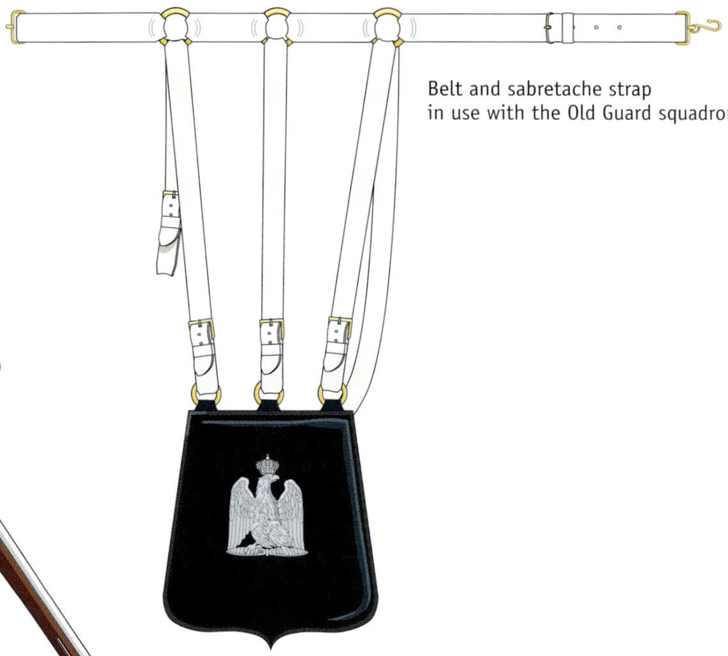

Belt and sabretache strap in use with the Old Guard squadron.

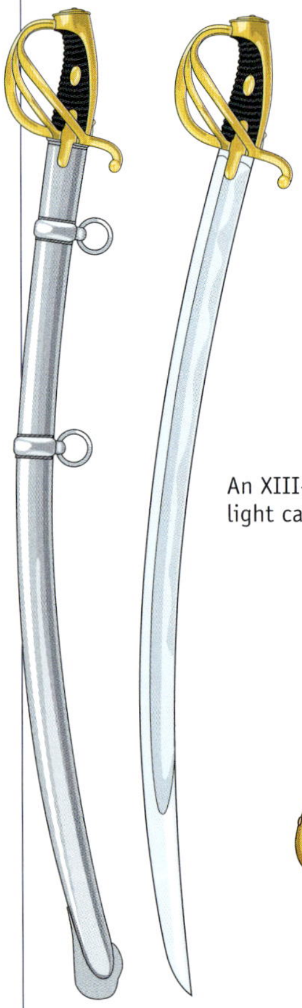

An XIII-model light cavalry sabre.

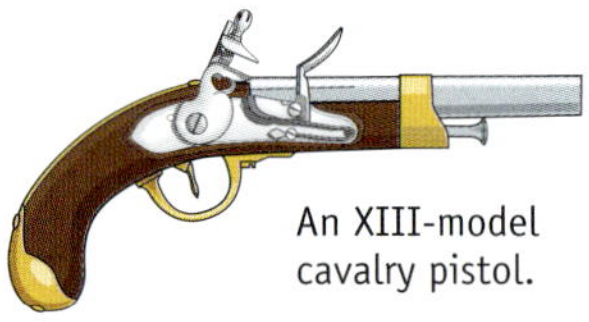

An XIII-model cavalry pistol.

An XIII-model cavalry musketoon.

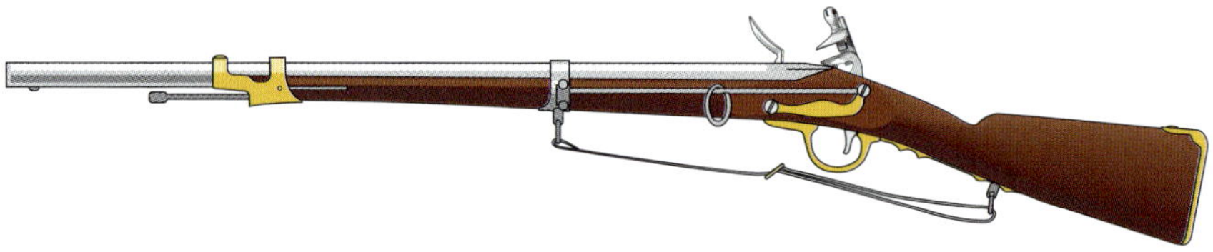

The 2nd Eclaireurs Regiment

The 2nd Eclaireurs Regiment of the Imperial Guard was also called the "Regiment of Eclaireurs-Dragons". Indeed, it was attached to the Dragoons of the Guard which supplied some of its men and officers.

Although the second decree for setting up the Eclaireurs stipulated that "[...] *the Second Regiment of Eclaireurs would be recruited with a levy of 1,000 men from the corners of the Empire* [...]", recruitment was the same as for the 1st Regiment. The only difference was the absence of the Gardes d'Honneur.

The cavalrymen coming from elements of the Old Guard were therefore the officers. Conscription and other units of the Line provided the rest: the 20th Dragoon Regiment and the 3rd and 7th Chevau-Legers Lancer Regiments. The 2nd Eclaireur Regiment was part of the Young Guard, except for the officers who came from the Old Guard.

The Eclaireurs-Dragons took part in the uninterrupted series of endless marches and battles during the Campaign for France until the end of March 1814. There were scarcely more than 200 troopers left in its ranks at that moment in the campaign. Its first commanding officer was Colonel Leclerc, who was quickly replaced by Colonel Hoffmayer from the 2nd Dragoon Regiment.

On 19 June 1814, at Poitiers, the regiment was disbanded by its commanding officer, Colonel-Major Hoffmayer. The remaining elements were transferred to the light cavalry of the Line.

The uniform of the Second Regiment

"The dress which would seem to suit the 2nd Eclaireurs is that of the Chevau-Legers Lancers of the Line; by adopting the same colour of habit-veste as that used by the Dragoons of the Guard, by adopting the Dragoons' lapels, the 2nd Eclaireurs would be distinguished and would resemble greatly the corps to which it belonged." [1]

As for the creation decree signed on 9 December, it shows quite vaguely that "the dress will be that of the Chasseurs of the Line".

The Shako

According to contemporary documentation, two types of shako were worn. One was an inverted, sawn-off cone with the same peak as the infantry shakos. It was about the same size as the Hussars' shako-rouleau. The other was the classic shako-rouleau with a flat visor.

These shakos were covered with crimson cloth and their upper circumference was surrounded by a cloth band with a string of black rings, or according to certain sources, a plain aurora stripe.

The cockade was held in place by an aurora (gold) braid loop and a brass button. A pompom the colour of the squadron, and a white plume for full dress, surmounted the whole.

The chinstrap comprised a small brass chain on a leather strip. An aurora cord was attached to the upper rear part of the shako and then worn saltire-wise, thus preventing the trooper from losing his hat. There was a black leather square at the rear of the hat to protect the nape.

The Coat

This was a coat with short tails (habit-veste) fastening down the front by means of 9 brass buttons. The collar, facings, turnbacks and piping were crimson. The shoulder flaps were green with crimson borders.

Trousers

These were cut from green cloth with a double crimson stripe down each side.

Other types were used: trousers made of green cloth buttoning on the side with a crimson stripe, lined with black calfskin; or trousers just like those worn by the 1st Regiment.

Equipment

This was made of white or black, unstitched buffalo hide and comprised a cartridge-case and its shoulder strap, and a musketoon-holder strap. The belt was the one used by the Chasseurs à Cheval of the Line.

Weapons

The ranks of Lancers were equipped with the 1812-model Lance and an An-XIII-model pistol hanging from the shoulder strap. The Carabinier ranks were armed with the An-XIII-model musketoon. All of them were armed with an An-XI-model light cavalry sabre.

Saddlery

Like the 1st Regiment, two types of saddles were used: the classic - Hungarian-style - model with a striped green schabrack; and the lighter version with leather panels, placed on a blanket. Both were presumably used as there is quite a lot of uncertainty about saddles.

The Trumpeters

They have something in common with most of the Trumpeters in the Guard: the colour of their uniform. The short-tailed coat was sky blue with a crimson distinctive, and a gold function stripe on his collar and facings.

Strangely enough, the Trompette-Major is wearing a coat cut according to the 1812 regulations, but with crimson lapels, after a drawing by E. Leliepvre which appeared in the magazine Le Passepoil.

The Officers

They wore the same uniform as the troopers but it was made of finer cloth with gold rank epaulettes. All the ornamentation on the shako was either gold trimming or gold metal.

The trousers were made of green cloth with a crimson side stripe. The buckles of the harness were gold. The schabrack was made of green cloth decorated with a single gold stripe. There was an eagle with gold trimmings in each corner.

If the Valmont Collection is to be believed, the Major (second colonel of the regiment), for instance, wore a coat with straight lapels. His epaulettes were made of a silver embroidered body and fringes with large twirls. All the trimmings on his equipment was green-striped gold.

1. A quotation taken from a report made to the Emperor on 7 December 1813, signed by General Drouot, in Raoul & Jean Brunon: *Garde Imperiale – Eclaireurs*, Presse de la Sopic, Marseille, 1961.

The 2nd Eclaireurs Regiment uniform

Shako.

Pelisse, seen from the front.

Pelisse, seen from the back.

Buttons.

Sash belt.

Habit-veste used by the Young Guard squadron.

Braces.

Breeches

Waistcoat.

Riding breeches.

Chasseur-style coat.

The Eclaireurs from the 2nd Regiment

NCO from the 2nd Eclaireur-Lancier Regiment.

Trooper from the 2nd Eclaireur Regiment wearing full dress, seen from the off-side.

Trooper from the 2nd Eclaireur Regiment wearing full dress, seen from the on-side.

The Eclaireurs from the Second Regiment

Eclaireur from the Second Regiment from the second rank, armed with a musketoon.

Eclaireur from the Second Regiment, according to a drawing by Lucien Rousselot.

Eclaireur from the Second Regiment, according to a drawing by H. Boisselier.

The Eclaireurs of the 2nd Regiment

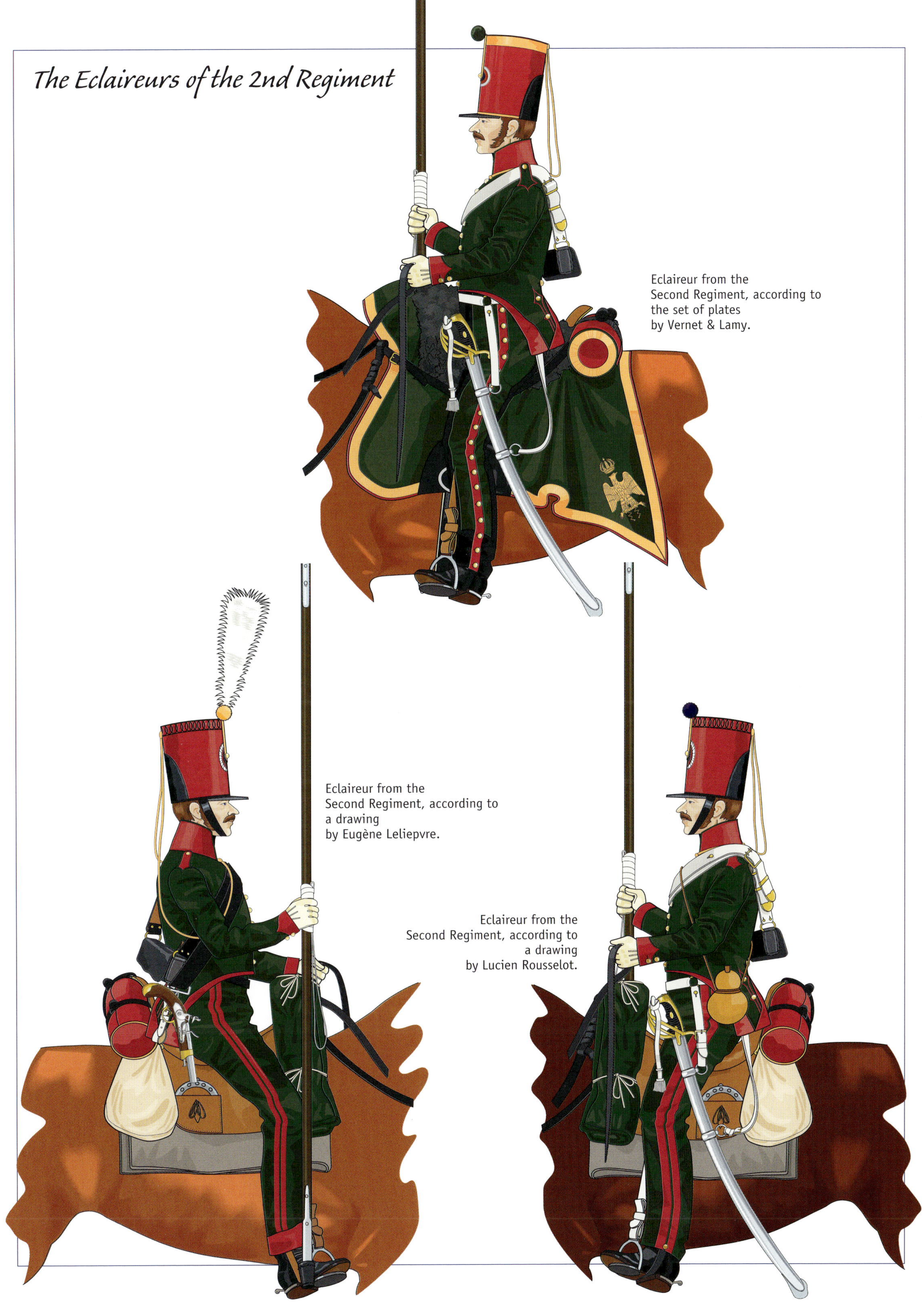

Eclaireur from the Second Regiment, according to the set of plates by Vernet & Lamy.

Eclaireur from the Second Regiment, according to a drawing by Eugène Leliepvre.

Eclaireur from the Second Regiment, according to a drawing by Lucien Rousselot.

The Troopers from the 2nd Regiment

Eclaireur from the Second Regiment, according to a drawing by H. Boisselier.

Eclaireur from the Second Regiment, according to the plates by Noirmont and Marbot.

Eclaireur from the Second Regiment according to the plates by Lienhart and Humbert. Note that the portmanteau braid is different from the saddlecloth's, as is the crown in the rear angle of the saddlecloth.

The Trumpeters of the 2nd Regiment

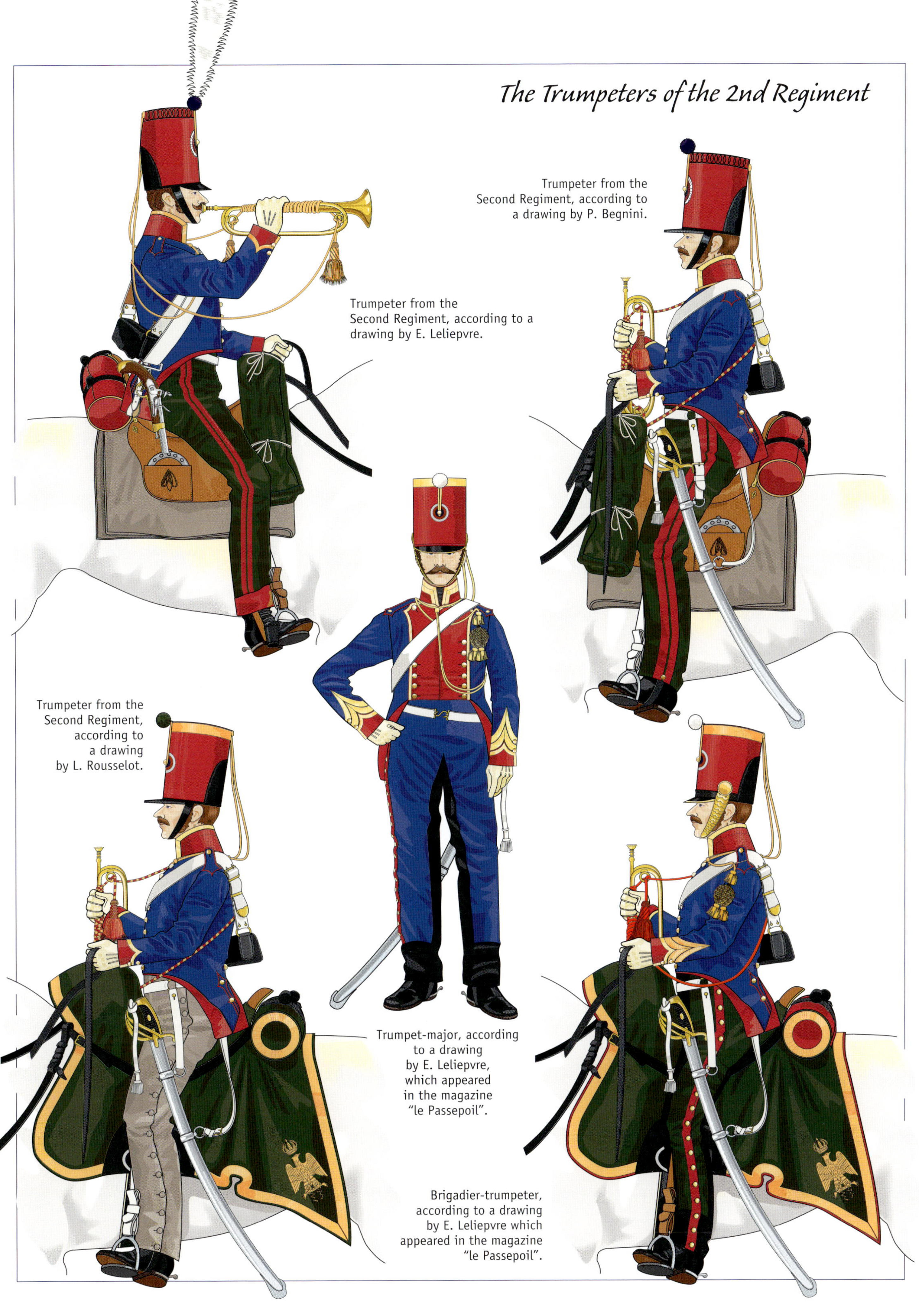

Trumpeter from the Second Regiment, according to a drawing by P. Begnini.

Trumpeter from the Second Regiment, according to a drawing by E. Leliepvre.

Trumpeter from the Second Regiment, according to a drawing by L. Rousselot.

Trumpet-major, according to a drawing by E. Leliepvre, which appeared in the magazine "le Passepoil".

Brigadier-trumpeter, according to a drawing by E. Leliepvre which appeared in the magazine "le Passepoil".

The Officers from the 2nd Eclaireurs Regiment

Colonel in second, according to a drawing by H. Boisselier.

Officer, according to a drawing by Eugène Leliepvre.

Junior officer, after the book by Raoul nd Jean Brunon given over to the Eclaireurs of the Guard.

The Eclaireur-Lanciers from the 3rd Regiment

Trooper from the 3rd Eclaireur-Lancier Regiment, according to a drawing by Lucien Rousselot.

Trooper from the 3rd Eclaireur-Lancier Regiment, according to a drawing by Lucien Rousselot.

Trooper from the 3rd Eclaireur-Lancier Regiment. This man, situated in the second rank, was armed with the cavalry musketoon and sabre.

The 3rd Eclaireur-lanciers Regiment

The 3rd Eclaireur Regiment was placed directly under the command of Major-General Krasinski, commanding the 1st Polish Chevau-Legers Regiment of the Guard to which they were attached.

As a result, no colonel was appointed and Squadron Commander Kozietulski was appointed Regimental Major by Napoleon. He set up the regiment in the Ave Maria quarter of Paris. The officers and the NCOs mostly came from the Old Guard and notably from the 1st Polish Chevau-Legers.

The troopers came from the last companies of the same regiment which were considered to be Young Guard. The strength was made up by men from the depot of the Polish corps at Sedan and subsequently by French recruits from the Courbevoie depot.

As and when they were formed, the 3rd Regiment squadrons joined the army; instruction of the new recruits continued on the way. The 3rd Eclaireur Regiment was part of General Pac's division which comprised the 1st Chevau-Legers, the Krakus and the Lithuanian Tartars. They fought on 11 February 1814 at Champaubert.

When Napoleon abdicated, the French troopers in the regiment were dismissed; the Poles were released from their oath and returned to Poland with elements of the 1st Chevau-Legers.

At the time of the dismissal, their strength stood at 46 officers and 551 troopers.

Uniform of the 3rd Eclaireur Regiment

The 3rd Regiment Eclaireurs' uniform was essentially the same as that of the 1st Chevau-Leger Regiment to which they were attached. But it was a lot cheaper. Besides there were some details which distinguished it from the Old Guard uniforms.

The Czapka

Although it was the same shape as the Old Guard's, it did cost only half the price. The shape and the attributes didn't change between 1807 and 1815; only its height was reduced by ¾ in (2 cm) from 8 ½ in (22 cm) to 7.8 in (20 cm).

The crown was covered with crimson cloth and its sides were fluted.

The imperial was criss-crossed with white Russian braid which was then tucked under it. The join between the crown and the sides was concealed by white thread braid on black velvet. On each side there were two silver quadrilobes with lion's heads and hooks. The visor was made of pressed leather; it had a gold metal edge.

AFTER DISBANDING

When they were disbanded, the Eclaireur squadrons were incorporated into the Chasseur and Hussar regiments according to the list below:

– The 1st Eclaireur Regiment
The 1st Squadron joined the 4th Chasseurs
The 2nd Squadron joined the 6th Chasseurs
The 3rd Squadron joined the 8th Chasseurs
The 4th Squadron joined the 12th Chasseurs

– The 2nd Eclaireur Regiment
The 5th Squadron joined the 2nd Hussars
The 6th Squadron joined the 5th Hussars
The 7th Squadron joined the 2nd Chasseurs
The 8th Squadron joined the 3rd Chasseurs

– The 3rd Eclaireur Regiment
Placed with the 1st Chevau-Legers Lancers and sent back to Russia.

The front of the hat was decorated with sunrays made of embossed brass whose silver centre showed an eagle sitting on four crossed lances in place of the crowned N. The hat was held in place by a chain chinstrap made of silver metal lined with crimson.

The tricolour cockade – with the white on the outside – contained a silver Maltese Cross. Coloured pompoms distinguished the squadrons.

The forage cap

Unlike the Lancers', the 1st Regiment's forage cap had a turban made of dark blue cloth with white braid. The pennant was crimson and four little white cords decorated it; it ended with a tassel, also white.

The Kurtka

There were no big differences compared with the one worn by the Old Guard, except for the quality of the cloth. The Polish Eclaireurs wore a pair of white woollen epaulettes. As for the conscripts, their shoulder flaps were blue with crimson borders. All of them wore a white cloth belt with three blue stripes that was fastened over the kurtka and hid the sabre holder belt.

Trousers

These were made of grey linen; there were no side stripes. There was black calfskin lining between the legs.

Equipment and Weapons

This was the same as for the 2nd Eclaireur Regiment. Weapons were issued in the same way as for the 1st and 2nd Regiments.

Saddlery

The Eclaireurs of the 3rd Regiment used the same saddles as the 1st and 2nd Regiments: the classic Hungarian-style and the lighter model with leather panels.

On the other hand, according to contemporary pictures and the supply reports, the different types of harnesses encountered seem to depend on the depot from which the Eclaireurs came from: sheepskin schabrack for the French conscripts from the Courbevoie depot, dark blue cloth schabrack for the Eclaireurs coming from the Polish troops general depot at Sedan.

The Trumpeters

Their czapkas were white, but they were decorated differently depending on the sources. Moreover, there were two types of kurtka: one was sky blue and the other white.

The latter was worn with blue trousers the same as those worn by the Chevau-Legers of the 1st Regiment but decorated on the side with blue cord between two white stripes.

This difference could be explained by the different origins of recruitment, but heir is no certainty on the matter.

The NCOs and Officers

These mostly came from the 1st Chevau-Leger Regiment. They kept their uniforms, equipment and weapons without any changes.

According to the iconography, no officers wearing campaign dress have been attested. Besides, it is not known whether junior officers from other units wore Polish-style uniforms.

The Troopers from the 3rd Regiment

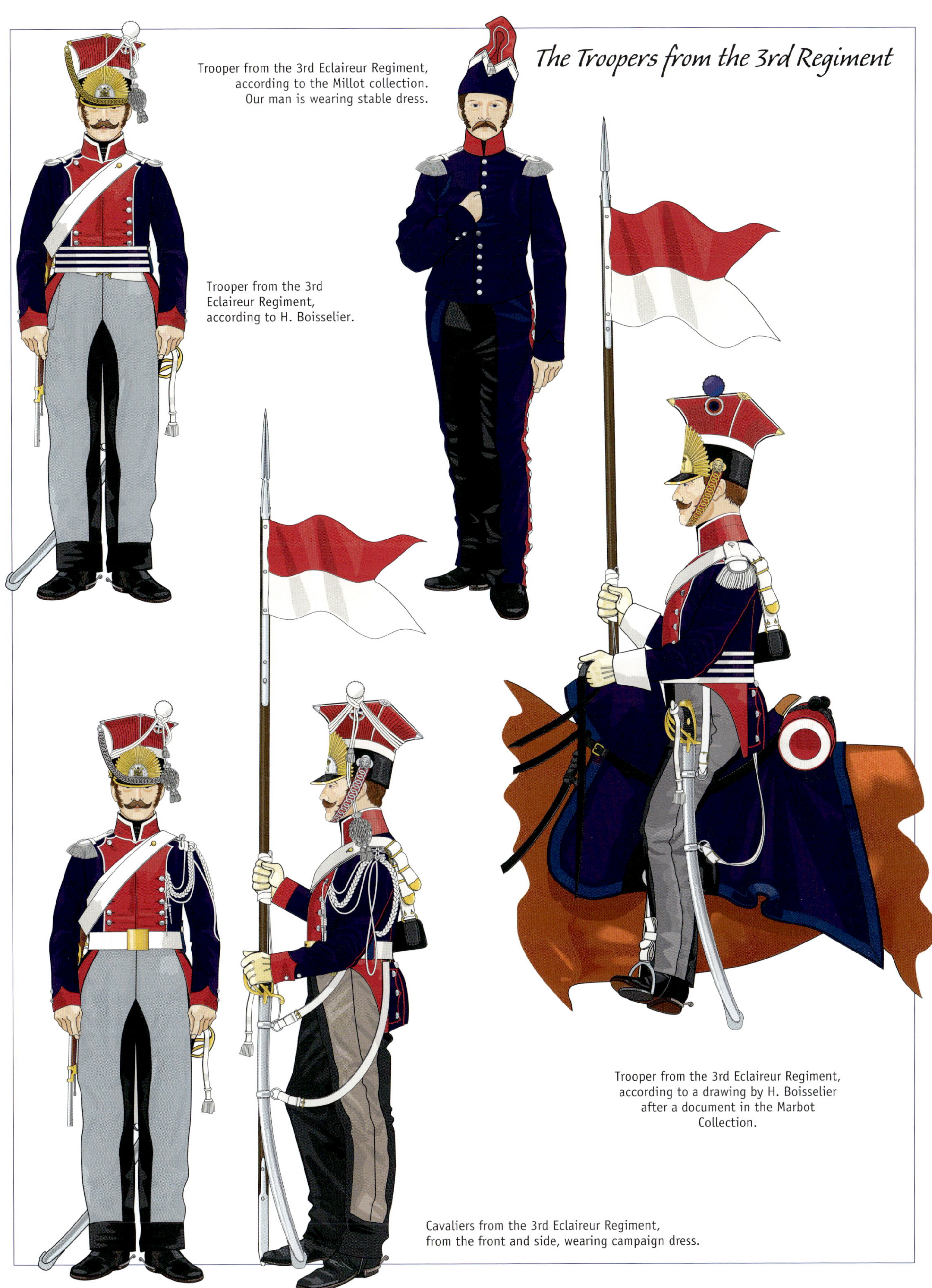

Trooper from the 3rd Eclaireur Regiment, according to the Millot collection. Our man is wearing stable dress.

Trooper from the 3rd Eclaireur Regiment, according to H. Boisselier.

Trooper from the 3rd Eclaireur Regiment, according to a drawing by H. Boisselier after a document in the Marbot Collection.

Cavaliers from the 3rd Eclaireur Regiment, from the front and side, wearing campaign dress.

The Trumpeters

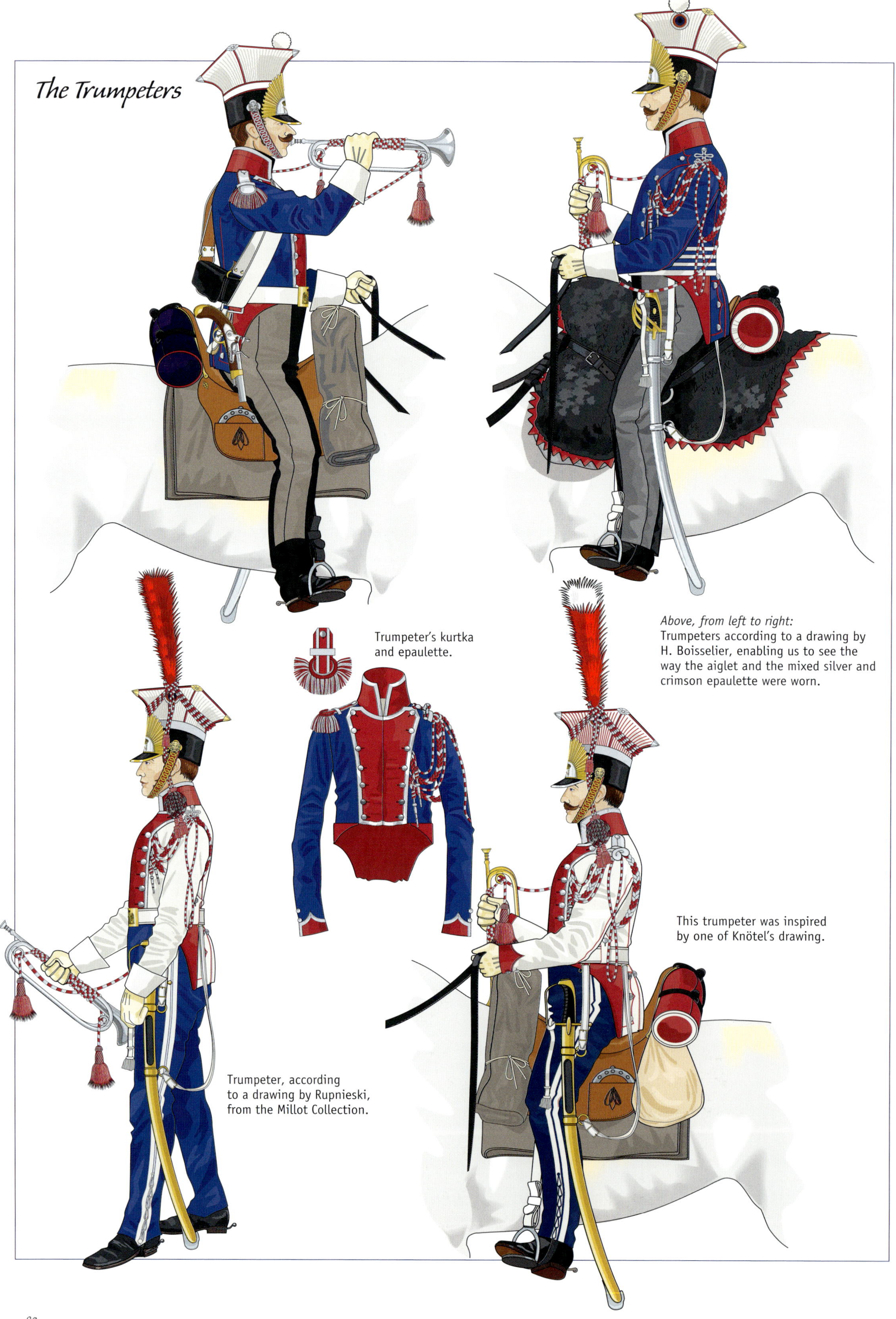

Trumpeter's kurtka and epaulette.

Above, from left to right:
Trumpeters according to a drawing by H. Boisselier, enabling us to see the way the aiglet and the mixed silver and crimson epaulette were worn.

This trumpeter was inspired by one of Knötel's drawing.

Trumpeter, according to a drawing by Rupnieski, from the Millot Collection.

The lithuanians Tartars

Trooper in 1812 in Lithuania, according to a documentary card by R. Forthoffer.

Trooper in 1813 during the German Campaign.

Trumpeters noted down by R. Forthoffer. They are from 1812 and were to be seen in Lithuania. We think however they apply more to the German Campaign in 1813, since the three trumpeters are wearing items from the Chevaux-légers of the Guard.

The lithuanian Tartars

Creating the Lithuanian Tartars and the Krakus, just like the Scouts, did actually correspond to a clear tactical need.

In 1812, the Lithuanian Tartars were set up, followed in 1813 by the Krakus.

All one has to do is read the Emperor's letters during the 1807 Campaign to understand how much the Cossacks worried him. Here are some extracts, among others:

"Landsberg, 18 February 1807, to General Duroc: [] *go ahead with the training of six hundred Polish Guards; I would very much like to have them in a month. Speak seriously to the Government and to Prince Poniatowski about organising 3 to 4,000 cavalry to counter the Cossacks* [].

"Landsberg, 20 February 1807, to General Duroc: [] *I have been informed that 900 Polish cavalry have reached Osterode; they will be my Cossacks. It would be a great help to the army if they were 3 or 4,000 of them* [].

During the campaign, Napoleon did not rest until he had raised some Polish cavalry regiments into the Line capable of confronting the Cossacks. But he also thought of his Guard.

In March 1807, he created the 1st Chevau-légers Regiment, followed by another in September 1810 and a third in July 1812.

In June 1812, Imperial troops occupied Lithuania. General van Hogendorp, Governor-General and aide-de-camp to Napoleon suggested levying a regiment from among the Muslim Tartars settled in Lithuania since the Middle Ages.

Officer from the lithuanian Tartars' squadron in 1813. *(Private Collection, RR)*

The idea was in fact put forward to him by Major Mustapha Mura Achmatowicz who proposed to recruit the unit himself, on the condition that it be part of the Imperial Guard. Since cavalry was needed to counter the Cossack threat, Napoleon accepted.

But the recruitment was not up to expectations and only one squadron was raised in October 1812. In December the same year, the Lithuanian Tartars were almost wiped out at Vilna trying to protect the French troops' retreat.

Achmatowicz was killed. The squadron's thirty survivors got through to the French lines at Posen led by Captain Samuel Hurzan Ulan.

In 1813, Ulan was allowed to raise a new Tartar regiment from among Russian prisoners, but in vain. He only succeeded in recruiting fifteen or so men in March 1813, Maréchal Bessières decided to incorporate what remained of the Tartar squadron, fifty men or so, into the remnants of the Third Regiment of Lithuanian Chevau-Légers of the Guard, crushed at Slomin in October 1812.

At the end, in December 1813, the Lithuanian Tartars and Chevau-Légers were attached to the 1st Polish Chevau-légers Regiment of the Guard, though still serving as distinct units. They took part in the German Campaign.

When the cavalry of the Guard was reorganised at the end of 1813, the Tartars, numbering scarcely forty troopers, were used as Eclaireurs-Lanciers and took part in the whole of the Campaign for France.

When Napoleon abdicated for the first time in April 1814, the forty survivors still under Captain Samuel Hurzan Ulan, were released from their oath. They returned to Lithuania with part of the 1st Chevau-Légers Regiment of the Guard under General Krasinski who rather ironically put the regiment at the disposal of the Tsar.

Uniforms and weapons

The oriental origins of these Muslim Tartars were reflected in their uniforms which were very similar to those of the Mamelukes on a lot of points: waistcoats with or without sleeves, baggy trousers taken in at the ankles, wide sash-belt, hat surrounded by a turban, etc.

The cut of some of the trousers does however reveal a certain Russian, even Cossack, influence. Islamic symbolism was present in the crescent decorating the hat and by some of the lance pennants which were half green and half white.

The weapons were also oriental: Turkish style scimitars, daggers, pistols (very likely the Caucasian type), and lances.

When the squadron was first set up, the colour and the uniform decorations must have been very varied but after April 1813, as reorganisation and re-equipment got under way, more conventional equipment and weapons were issued to the Lithuanian Tartars who nonetheless managed to hold on to their ever so characteristic appearance.

Some items of their uniforms were even made by Parisian tailors: after all they did belong to the Guard.

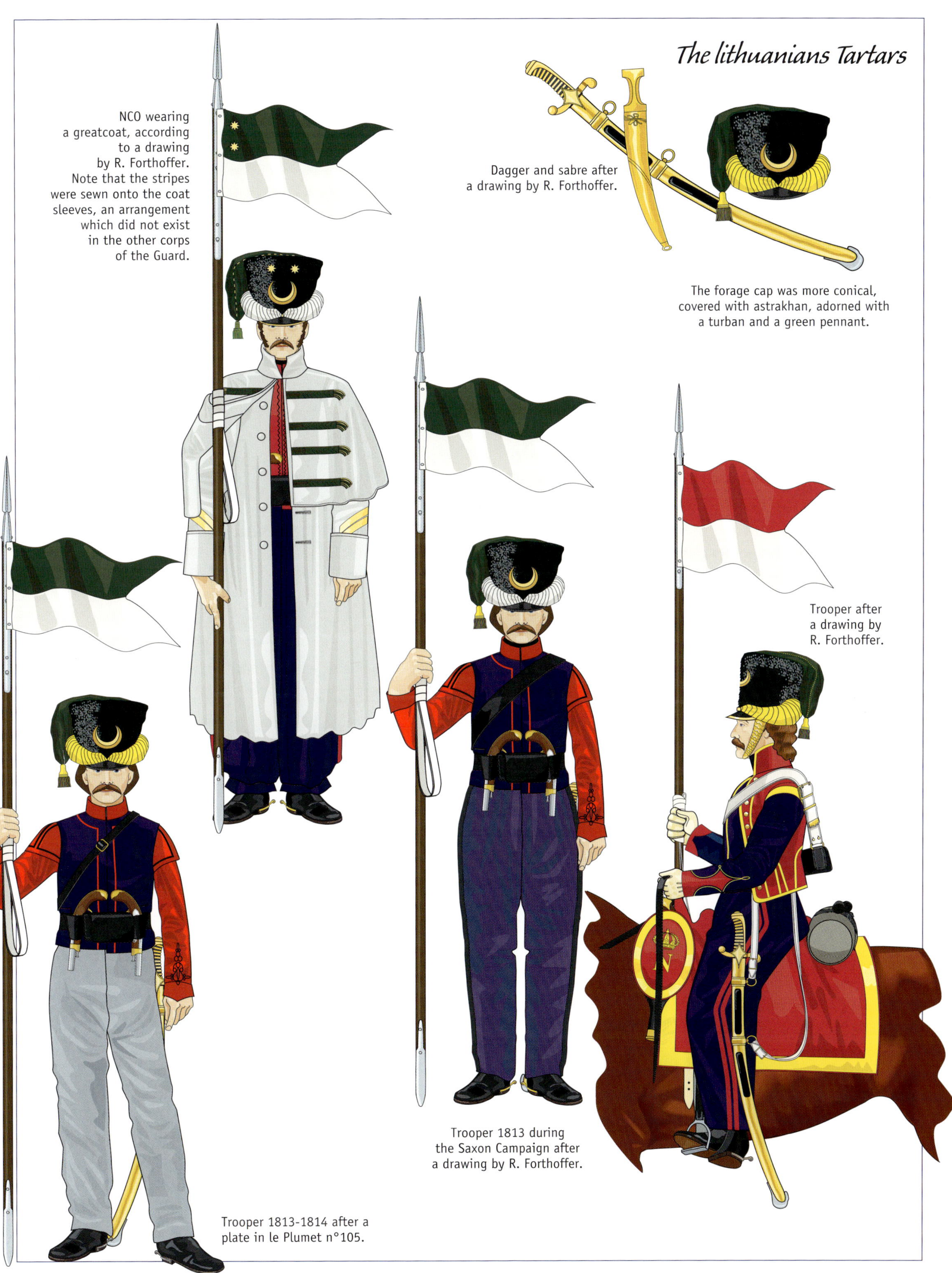
The lithuanians Tartars

NCO wearing a greatcoat, according to a drawing by R. Forthoffer. Note that the stripes were sewn onto the coat sleeves, an arrangement which did not exist in the other corps of the Guard.

Dagger and sabre after a drawing by R. Forthoffer.

The forage cap was more conical, covered with astrakhan, adorned with a turban and a green pennant.

Trooper after a drawing by R. Forthoffer.

Trooper 1813 during the Saxon Campaign after a drawing by R. Forthoffer.

Trooper 1813-1814 after a plate in le Plumet n°105.

The lithuanians Tartars
Officer, according to
documentary card
by R. Forthoffer.
Officer, according to a plate
by Noirmont and Marbot
with a Cossack forage cap.
Trooper in the 1813
Campaign.
Officer
at the Battle
of Leipzig,
according
to a plate
by Rigo.
Trooper in the 1813
Campaign.

The Polish Krakus

Trooper from the initial units in January 1813

Krakus from the later units after a plate by R. Moravski.

A Krakus wearing a Polish forage cap. He is armed with a lance and a pair of pistols in the saddle holsters.

Officer wearing service dress in 1813 after a drawing by R. Moravski.

The Polish Krakus

In December 1812, Napoleon returned to Paris in haste. The leftovers of the *Grande Armée* were starting to arrive in Prussia and in Poland in a sorry state.

A new regiment

Poniatowski tried to reorganise an army of the Duchy of Warsaw, but the government abandoned the capital and withdrew to Krakow at the beginning of 1813, because the Russians were advancing through Polish territory.

The organisation went quickly and in April 1813, Prince Poniatowski was able to review his new troops. Among the 4,000 troopers who filed past him, people noticed the splendid uniform of a new regiment: the Krakus.

This regiment had been organised by a decree dated 19 December 1812 and was formed in the Krakow region with local recruits. Every fifty households had to furnish one trooper equipped, mounted and armed on a little peasant horse called a *konia*. Each trooper received a 15 gulden bonus on top of his pay. Major Rzuchowski was in command of this new unit, made up of four squadrons.

On 27 June 1813, the initial part of the campaign had just finished, ending with the Pleisswitz Armistice, and the Duchy of Warsaw army was able to join the French army. In a decree dated the 27th, Napoleon finalised the organisation of Poniatowski's troops, into the 8th Corps of the Imperial Army. In this corps, a small, separate unit was set up using the leftovers of the 14th Cuirassiers (Colonel Dziebonski) and the regiment of Krakus. General Uminski commanded this little brigade which furnished the Prince with his usual escort.

The 8th Corps was at Zittau where the Emperor came to inspect them. He noticed the Krakus and was inspired by this type of unit when creating the Eclaireurs of the Guard.

On 17 August 1813, Blücher broke the armistice. Poniatowski was sent back to Waldheim to cover the army's communications, marching to the rescue of Lefebvre-Desnouettes who had been pushed about by Platov's Cossack raids, supported by the first Saxon turncoat, General Thieldmann.

Following the death of Poniatowski, the Poles remained loyal to the Emperor who, in a whirl of new measures and decrees, tried to organise the troops left over after this disaster. The Polish Corps reformed at Sedan, under the leadership of Dombrowski, then of Pac. Two Lancer regiments were ready, and Dwernick's infantrymen were made into Krakus. Pac was able to lead 800 troopers.

1814... the invasion, and the beginning of the fantastic Campaign for France, a masterpiece of courage and will. Pac's men marched with the Guard. They distinguished themselves at Berry-au-Bac on 5 March, at Craonne on the 6th and Laon on the 9th of the same month. Then followed the Battle of Paris, and here again the Dwernicki's Krakus distinguished themselves. These Cracovian peasants had therefore remained faithful right up to the end.

KRAKUS AT WAR WITH PONIATOWSKI

Poniatowski waged a remarkable partisan war against this enemy, covering himself with glory at Frohburg, Poenig, Chemnitz and Altenburg.

16 October 1813 was the first day of the Battle of Leipzig. The Poles distinguished themselves and the same evening, on the battlefield, Napoleon made Prince Poniatowski a Maréchal de France.

On the 17th, fighting stopped and the Emperor stiffened his set up and had his convoys cross the Elster. The 8th Corps was on the right of the Army, at Dolotz on the Pleisse. The day was terrible, but although outnumbered, despite the Saxons' defection and heavy losses, the allies were marking time. Ammunition, however, was running low, the park had not joined them; Napoleon had to decide to retreat. During the night, the corps crossed the bridge over the Elster calmly. The 8th Corps crossed in turn, but Poniatowski stayed behind with his small cuirassier and Krakus escort to form the rearguard.

Other troops were still covering Leipzig: towards the south, with the Poles, were MacDonald and Lauriston. Rosenthal in the suburbs; Reynier headed the Durutte Division. Dombrowski was entrenched in the Halle suburb. Ney was still to the east.

On the morning of the 19th, the renegades attacked the French army which was getting away from them. The rearguard troops held out. The attackers' losses were huge, but it was at that moment that a fatal mistake was made: the Lindenau bridge blew up before it should have done, cutting off the last defenders in Leipzig.

The news hadn't reached the others in the south yet. Poniatowski charged like a simple soldier amongst his Krakus and cuirassiers, but this handful of men couldn't hold out forever.

The Prince was wounded in the arm for the third time in as many days. MacDonald crossed the Pleisse with the headquarters, throwing his horse into the river. It was only then that Poniatowski thought about retreating. In turn he threw himself into the river, but his wounded arm hindered him and without Captain Bléchamps (one of his aides), he'd have drowned. Once they reached the other side of the Pleisse, Poniatowski and his escort learned of the bridge's destruction. They'd have to swim across the Elster, too.

The enemy rushed up on all sides and suddenly a projectile hit the Prince and threw him down unconscious. His comrades brought him round and tried to look after him, but this was to accept being taken prisoner. Poniatowski got up and declared in a weak voice: "God entrusted me with the Poles' honour, I'll give it back only to God. He headed for the Elster and threw his white horse into the current, but he didn't have the strength and was carried off. Captain Bléchamps tried to save him again. He brought him back up to the surface several times but the current was too strong and both men disappeared and drowned."

Docteur François Guy Hourtoulle
in L'épopée napoléonienne

The Krakus' uniform

It seems that the 1813 and 1814 uniforms were slightly different. Here are the two versions known to us.

In the book by Chalminski and Malibran which gave a lot of information about the Krakus, a plate reproduces the uniform as Colonel Bialkowski describes it in his memoirs. Here is that description:

- Melon-shaped crimson forage cap with round the base a band of black astrakhan. White piping in each fold. Above, an ornamental oval made of white braid surrounded by slender *à la tcherkesse*. On the left-hand side a cockade with a white plume.
- Coat in the form of an overcoat, instead of a kurtka. Coat reaching down to the knees, made of dark blue cloth; crimson collar and facings, white piping on all the seams.
- Instead of the cartridge pouch, there was a metal Cherkassy cartridge pocket on either side of the chest, with five compartments, each with a cover linked by a small chain to a button on the coat. Each cartridge clip was surrounded by white braid, silver for the officers.
- Dark blue trousers with a very narrow crimson band, with leather between the legs.
- Instead of a coat, a very loose cape with sleeves, made of grey cloth with a collar falling down onto the shoulders and a hood which was big enough to cover the head if it rained.
- Crimson belt.
- Pennant-less lance, sabre and pistol.
- No trumpet, but "Bunczuncks", a sort of half lance garnished with a horsetail at the top, like the Turks' toug. It was with these tougs that the men communicated with each other silently at a distance, to avoid alerting the enemy.

The horse equipment was dark blue with a crimson edge, the portmanteau as well.

For the officers, silver replaced the white, a schabrack made of dark blue cloth with a silver edge, and a seat made of black astrakhan

The Polish Krakus

Officer, according to a drawing by J. Girbal in Dr Hourtoulle's collection of plates.

Junior officer wearing ordinary service dress in 1814, according to a drawing by Rupniewski.

Junior officer from the Sedan depot, in 1814 after a plate by Moraski.

Senior officer from the Sedan depot in 1814 after a plate by Moraski.

Officer, according to a drawing by J. Girbal in Dr Hourtoulle's collection of plates.

The Horse Artillery

Going back directly to the gunner companies of Bonaparte's Guides during the Egyptian Campaign, the Horse Artillery was incorporated into the Consular Guard (Garde des Consuls), adapting the *à la hussarde* dress to the blue of the Artillery. The decree dated 28 November 1799 set up an artillery company assigned to the Consular Guards to serve the guns of the newly created unit.

The 13 Nivose An VIII decree fixed its strength at 110 men (40 gunners, first class and 52, second class), officers and NCOs included, for eight guns.

On 8 September 1800, the company was increased to 157 men now serving 12 cannons.

A light artillery squadron with two companies and an HQ replaced this first unit on 8 March 1802. On 11 Brumaire An X, a new decree organised the Artillery of the Consular Guard's materiel into four divisions, of which one was in the reserve. This squadron became a regiment on 15 April 1806, made up of three two-company squadrons, each with a strength of 97 men to which were added 25 Velites.

When the Foot Artillery was created in 1808 (see Volume One of the collection), the Horse Artillery was reduced to two two-company squadrons.

When the Guard was reorganised in 1813, the regiment was increased to three two-company squadrons and the number of cannon from 120 to 190, shared out among 26 batteries.

A Horse Artillery company of the Young Guard was created at the end of 1813. In July 1814, the regiment was disbanded only to be recreated in 1815 with four companies of four six-gun batteries.

The gunners' height was fixed at 5 feet 6 inches (1.81 m) in 1805 and was reduced 5 ft 5 in a few years later.

Gunner from the Horse Artillery in the Consular Guard wearing the *à la hussarde* dress and the shako, around 1800. *(Oil by Baron Lejeune, Private Collection, RR)*

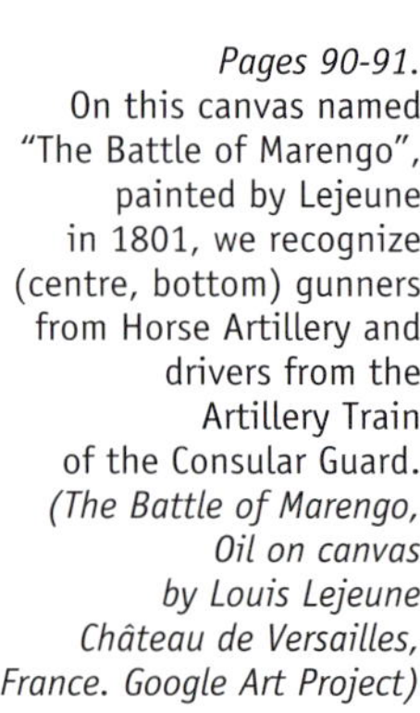

Pages 90-91. On this canvas named "The Battle of Marengo", painted by Lejeune in 1801, we recognize (centre, bottom) gunners from Horse Artillery and drivers from the Artillery Train of the Consular Guard. *(The Battle of Marengo, Oil on canvas by Louis Lejeune Château de Versailles, France. Google Art Project)*

Uniforms under the Consular Guard

What the gunners in the Consular Guard wore is not very well-known and the rare pictures that have come down to us do not help very much[1]. Several objects and some supply lists and returns are known to us and we are able to give a description of the overall picture of the Artilleryman.

The gunner in the Guard had an *à la hussarde* uniform made up of a dolman, the traditional sash belt, the Hungarian-style breeches or riding breeches. He wore a small-sized dolman, probably the same as that of the Chasseurs à Cheval of the Consular Guard. A cartridge pouch, a belt, a sabre and a sabretache, all from the Light Cavalry made up the uniform. A long coat with aglets worn over a waistcoat, plaited or plain – the same model as the Chasseurs à Cheval – was also in use.

The *à la chasseur* coat and the bearskin – resembling closely that of the Grenadiers à Cheval – could be worn by the gunners attached to the foot soldiers of the Guard. This bearskin hat had no background colour or plate. A double plaited cord ending in flounders was worn on the right hand rear side of the headdress, and on the left-hand side, were the plume and the cockade.

The *à la hussarde* dress was probably worn by the men assigned to the mounted troops.[2]

Some sources evoke a shako without giving any details whether it was a shako with fur – therefore a colback – or a shako made of black velvet with a visor, with a red and black pennant edged and decorated with black interlacing.[3]

"A la hussarde"

In September 1800, the uniform – this time determined by adopting the Hussar dress for the Chasseurs à Cheval – evolved a little.

The dolman was dark blue with a blue collar and pointed scarlet facings. The plaits, the Russian braid and the cord forming the buttonholes were made of red wool. Three rows of 18 yellow buttons fastened and decorated the dolman.

The scarlet belt had yellow loops, like the attaching cords. The blue waistcoat was edged with scarlet, its square cord was the same; three rows of small yellow buttons fastened it.

(continued on page 93)

1. Two watercolours by General Lejeune painted during the summer of 1800, and several gunners visible on the canvas entitled the "Battle of Marengo" by the same painter, dated 1801; finally, a gunner painted by Hoffmann and published in 1924 in the Carnets de la Sabretache.

2. *In* Lucien Rousselot *in « Les uniformes de l'armée française ».*

3. Like the one that Gunner Herley was wearing in Lejeune's watercolour.

Embroidered first model of sabretache.

Second model of sabretache, made of cut out brass.

Horse artilleryman wearing full dress, according to Plate n°60 by L. Rousselot.

The Horse Artillery remounts were dark bays or black horses.

Gunners

Gunner wearing undress service uniform.

1st Class Gunner, according to L. Rousselot.

Canonnier Wearing coat after L. Rousselot.

Gunner in 1806-1807, according to L. Rousselot.

Gunner in about 1807, according to the Weiland Manuscript.

Gunner wearing a pelisse. Only the waistcoat was worn under the pelisse; it was so tight-fitting, there was no room to wear the dolman and the sash underneath it.

CAMPAIGN DRESS

There was no properly defined campaign dress before 1810. For example, in 1805 and 1809, the gunners wore their pelisse normally, over the plain or braided waistcoat, whereas for the Prussian and Polish Campaigns, they had to wear the long *à la française* coat.

During the second half of the period, the Horse Artillerymen went off campaigning wearing a dolman. In 1813, the pelisses were withdrawn without anybody wearing them. They were stocked for too long a time in the warehouses, which made them unsuitable for use; only a small number were used, after they were refurbished.

(continued from page 88)

There was another waistcoat, this time double breasted with two rows of buttons which was worn with a long French-style coat, also blue. Its collar and pointed lapels were blue; the pointed facings, the turnbacks, the edge of the collar, the lapels and Russian braid pockets were all scarlet.

The grenades on the turnbacks were blue. All the buttons were yellow. The shoulder trefoils, like the aglets were red. The Hungarian breeches were blue; their flat braid forming Hungarian knots was red. The black sheepskin leather riding breeches were blue and their seam stripes were scarlet; they were decorated with yellow buttons.

THE UNIFORM DURING THE EMPIRE

Until the Guard was disbanded in 1814, the items of clothing did not change very much and the way they were worn together remained was the same.

The busby (colback)

The busby, like the one worn by the Chasseurs à cheval, was made of black fur. Adopted during the Consular period, it remained almost unchanged until the end of the Empire. A short-lived visor appeared in 1801, it was removed in 1801. In the same year, the busby became more voluminous.

At first it was rather narrow and was adorned with a pennon on the right-hand side, long, scarlet ending in a tassel. On the left were the plume and the cockade. The cord at first with two strands - one simple and the other plaited - then a single one, disappeared in 1809. The cord was then reduced to its simplest expression and only comprised two flounders ending in tassels.

The plume was scarlet, the cockade was tricolour, made at first of cloth replaced in around 1804 by a chenille cockade displaying the letter N embroidered on the blue centre. In campaign or marching dress, the busby's scarlet pennon was tucked inside and covered with a waxed cloth roundel.

The hat (bicorn)

The hat was worn from the corps' creation for town dress with the coat, the dolman alone or wearing the pelisse. The hat had a braid cockade, loose twists - in the corners - and little scarlet cords. A more flexible plume than that on the busby could be attached to the cockade.

The forage cap

This was blue. The braid, the grenade on the turban, like the edging and the tassel on the pennon, were made of scarlet wool.

The dolman

The dolman belonging to the brigadiers and the gunners had three rows of buttons. It was identical to the one from the previous era.

The pelisse

A blue pelisse lined with white flannel appeared in 1801. It was garnished with black lambskin and had the same tresses, square cord, Russian braid and buttons as the dolman.

The pelisse was usually worn loose over the left-hand shoulder with the dolman, or over the waistcoat. It had three rows of buttons.

The waistcoats

The straight waistcoat was blue with scarlet braid and cord. It had three rows of 15 little buttons. There was also a plain blue waistcoat; it was double breasted with two rows of buttons and edged with scarlet after 1813.

The sash-belt

The sash-belt, like the one worn during the Consular period, was made up of a red tangle garnished with loops, an olive and yellow fastening cord.

The *à la chasseur* coat

When wearing undress uniform - marching or campaign, the gunners wore a long *à la chasseur* coat. A trefoil aglet was placed on the left-hand shoulder, the right-hand one being decorated with a trefoil made of trimmings, both being made of red wool.

Thin strips of scarlet cloth held them in place. The cut of this item evolved like those worn in the other corps of the Guard; the skirts became shorter and the fit closer.

During the Prussian and Polish Campaigns, the coat was probably worn over the braided waistcoat and the Hungarian breeches. It was usually worn with the plain waistcoat and the riding breeches.

The greatcoat-cloak

The greatcoat-cloak with a collar and a cape was blue. It was double-breasted and was fitted with two rows of seven buttons.

Exercise and stable dress

The stable jacket was blue; it had sleeves and was decorated with two rows of bone buttons. The camisole with sleeves was made of blue cloth and was used for instruction and exercises.

It was double-breasted and was fastened with two rows of seven buttons. There were two further buttons on each sleeve.

The Hungarian breeches

During the whole period, the Hungarian breeches were decorated with two Hungarian knots at the opening of the fly and a tress on the side seams.

(continued on page 96)

Gunners
Gunner in social dress,
according to L. Rousselot.
Brigadier wearing
campaign dress towards
the end of the Empire.
Brigadier wearing
campaign dress towards
the end of the Empire.
Gunner in summer
social dress.
Gunner servant
supplier wearing
exercise dress.
Artilleryman from
the Young Guard in
around 1814.
Shako of the
Young Guard.
Gunner,
according to
Henschel in
about 1807.
Model of sabretache
from the end
of the Empire.

Uniform
Dolman and buttons.
Forage cap.
Colback.
Pelisse.
Sash belt.
Straps.
Pelisse, front view
Waistcoats.
Shirt.
Longjohns.
Aglet.
Hat.
Breeches.
Riding breeches.
Overcoat and *à la chasseur* coat.
Rank stripes, from left to right:
1. Gunner with a 10 years' service chevron
2. Gunner, First Class with 10 to 20 years' service.
3. Brigadier with 25 years' seniority.
4. Maréchal des Logis
5. Maréchal des Logis Chef.
6. Adjudant.
1
2
3
4
5
6

(continued from page 93)

The riding breeches

The riding breeches remained the same from the beginning of the Consulate to the end of the Empire with the same cut and decorations. They were blue and had black leather padding on the inside of the thighs; there was a red stripe on each side, decorated with eighteen copper buttons.

The boots

The Hungarian boots had a border with a heart and a tassel, both scarlet. The spurs were made of bronzed iron. When the Imperial Guard was reformed in 1815, the Horse Artillery received new uniform items before setting off for Belgium.

The Hussar-style dress was not tailored and the artillerymen received long French-style coats with aglets, corded waistcoats, riding breeches, greatcoat-cloaks, forage caps and stable jackets, colbacks fitted with their cockades and plumes, portmanteaus, cartridge cases, buffalo-hide belts and knots.

The cartridge cases

The cartridge case was made of varnished leather; its flap was cut out en accolade and was at first decorated with a grenade then, after 1806, with a crowned eagle placed over two cannon. This was stamped out of brass.

The leatherwork

Since 1801, all the leatherwork (cartridge case straps, belt, sabretache straps and belts) was made of white buffalo hide stitched along the edges. The decorations on the bandoleer, the buckles, loops and rings were made of polished, browned brass.

The sabretache

This was blue with a wide red stripe. In the centre there was a gold yellow woollen grenade, surrounded by embroidered plain leaves surmounted with a white band on which was inscribed "Garde des Consuls".

his item of equipment was replaced in 1805 by another model of the same colour and makeup but now decorated with a crowned eagle and two crossed cannon surrounded by leaves, everything still made of plain embroidery.

This very beautiful but costly sabretache was replaced probably in 1811 by a model whose decoration was made of stamped brass. When marching, the gunner protected his sabretache with a black leather sheath, probably in 1809. In 1812 a crowned brass eagle decorated the sheath.

The sabre

The Light Cavalry An-XII (1804-1805) model sabre gradually replaced the hussar sabre of the Consular period. The red wool sabre-knot was replaced in 1806 by one made of white buffalo hide ending with a red tassel.

The harnesses

During the Consulate, the *à la hussarde* saddle had panels. Its quarters were made of leather with pommel and cantle circled with brass. It was covered with a sheepskin schabrack which was kept by the troopers for the undress uniform until 1808 whereas the blue wool schabrack edged with scarlet was used for full dress.

The portmanteau

After 1800, this was scarlet edged ends. A stripe of the same colour decorated the bottom.

The schabrack

During the Consular period, the gunners used a sheepskin schabrack. Schabracks made of blue cloth were decorated with grenades during the Consulate and apparently issued to the NCOs and brigadiers. The blue cloth schabracks were first used for parades then were issued from 1806 onwards to the whole regiment. The gunners used their old sheepskin schabracks.

The Polish Campaign probably marked the end of the joint use of both models of schabracks. The blue cloth schabrack, edged and decorated in red, was decorated with grenades ever since it appeared. The scarlet stripe used was wider than the one sewn on the other Imperial Guard schabracks.

The head harness

In 1801, the bridle headstall received a sun on the small cross but kept its crescent throat latch and its brass buckles. The bit had studs stamped with a grenade. The sun could also be seen on the saddle breatspiece.

The ordinary netting was made of black leather as were the reins.

These items were replaced by red wool netting. The head harness also comprised the parade headstall, festooned with scarlet along its edges, and a breast lunge.

During the Hundred Days, the gunners received brand new schabracks and harnesses, like those described above.

The Artillery Horses

The horses' robe was preferably dark (bay or black) during the Consulate and at the beginning of the Empire, before being black only with the 1806 reorganisation.

In 1812, the administration made a list of a whole variety of shades of black coats: dyed matt black, plain black, jay black, jay rubican black and plain black zain.

The Second Gunners

The gunners in the 3rd Squadron were called the "second gunners" after the 1813 reorganisation. They received no pelisse, nor hat nor coat. Their cheaper leatherwork had no stitching along the edges. The officers in this squadron were from the Old Guard.

The Young Guard Company

A company of the Young Guard was formed at the end of 1813. These artillerymen received an overcoat without aglets, a plain waistcoat, a greatcoat-cloak, a stable jacket, a forage cap, stable trousers, a portmanteau, riding breeches, a shako with cord and pompom, a shako cover, boots, gloves, a belt,

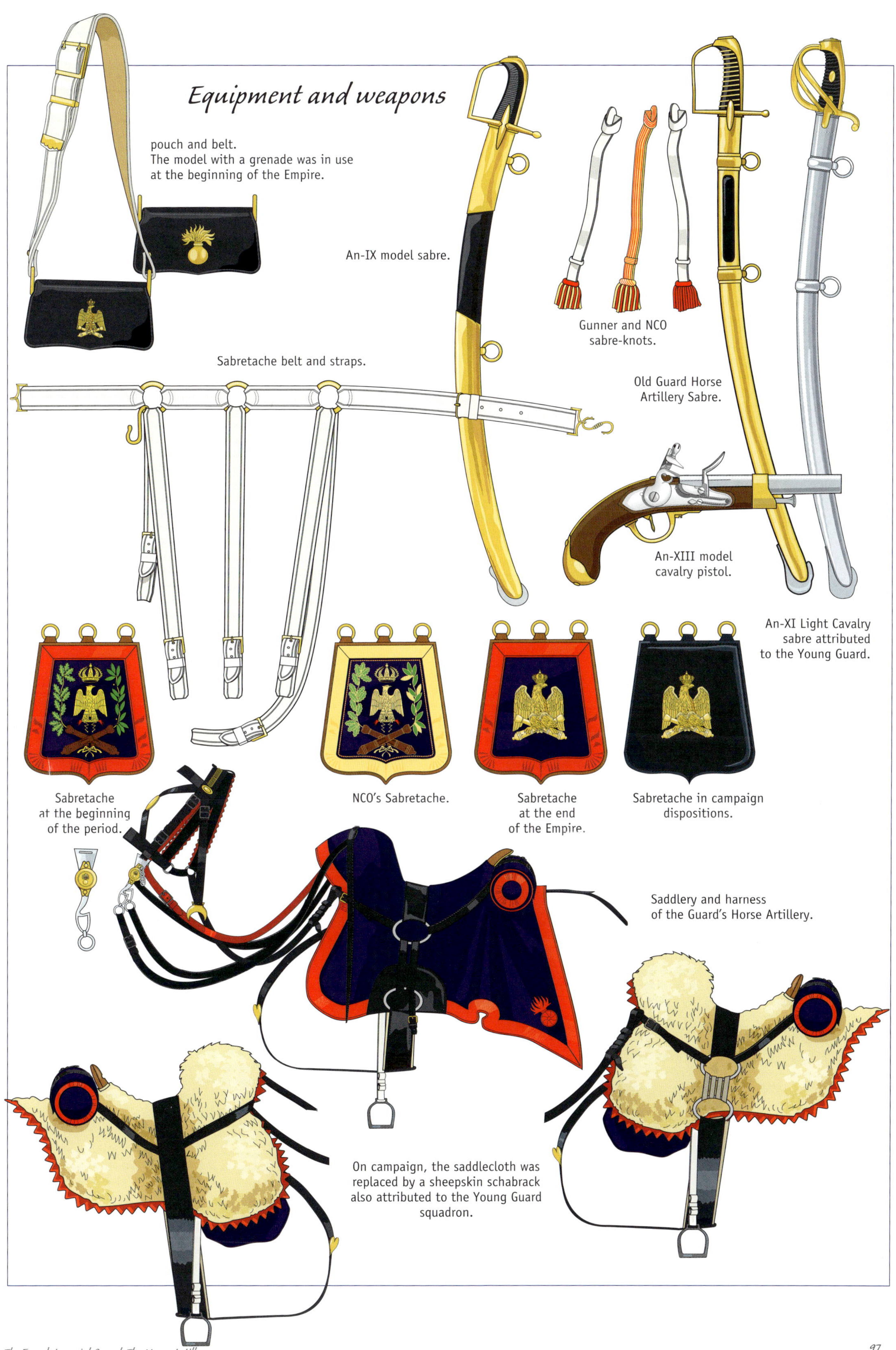
Equipment and weapons
pouch and belt.
The model with a grenade was in use
at the beginning of the Empire.
An-IX model sabre.
Gunner and NCO
sabre-knots.
Sabretache belt and straps.
Old Guard Horse
Artillery Sabre.
An-XIII model
cavalry pistol.
An-XI Light Cavalry
sabre attributed
to the Young Guard.
Sabretache
at the beginning
of the period.
NCO's Sabretache.
Sabretache
at the end
of the Empire.
Sabretache in campaign
dispositions.
Saddlery and harness
of the Guard's Horse Artillery.
On campaign, the saddlecloth was
replaced by a sheepskin schabrack
also attributed to the Young Guard
squadron.

a cartridge case and its strap, a knot, a skin schabrack, a leather saddle, bridles and accessories.

The leatherwork issued to the troopers of the company had no stitching, like the Artillery of the Line model. The horses had a variety of coats as with the other mounted units of the Young Guard.

The marks of rank and seniority

The brigadiers wore a uniform which was identical to that of the rest of the troopers; only two aurora wool chevrons worn on the sleeves of the dolman, pelisses and coats distinguished them for the others.

The gunner, first class, wore the same stripes as the brigadiers but on the left sleeve only.

Seniority chevrons were made of aurora wool.

The NCOs' uniforms

The dolman and the pelisse were garnished with five rows of buttons. The trimmings, flat tresses, square cord, Russian braid, olive and pelisse cord were mixed one third gold and two thirds red wool. The pelisse was no longer edged with black fur but with brown or russet marmot or fox back fur. The loops, olive, cord and belt tassels, flat tress on the breeches, edging and tassel on the boots, cords, flounders and colback tassels, as well as the Russian braid and the pennon tassel, as with the waistcoat braiding, were all made of the same proportions of gold and red wool.

The waistcoat, like the dolman and the pelisse, had five rows of yellow buttons. The *à la chasseur* coat was the same as that of the troopers but made of better quality cloth. The grenades on the turnbacks were gold; the aglet worn on the left, like the distinctives on the coat, was one third gold and two thirds red wool.

On the right, the trefoil was made of gold braid lined with red. *"A red disk was placed in the centre of each buckle"*.[4] The shoulder flaps were probably made of red cloth. This disposition was common to all the NCOs no matter what the rank. When wearing undress uniform, the NCOs could wear a blue double-breasted frock coat.

The hat had a gold cockade cord, the little cords and the loose twists in the corners were mixed red and gold. The forage cap was the same as the troopers'.

The NCOs' sabre knot was trimmed in gold and red, whereas that of the white buffalo hide was issued. Only the tassel was mixed gold and red.

Gunner from Horse Artillery in the Consular Guard, around 1800. *(Watercolour of Maurice Orange, Private Collection, RR)*

4. *In* Lucien Rousselot *in « Les uniformes de l'armée française ».*

The sabretache

The wonderful sabretache was edged with festooned *à la soubise* gold braid. An aurora Russian braid edged on the inside with a little gold cord doubled up the braid.

The ornaments were those of the troopers enhanced with gold. The eagle on the decorations was embroidered as was the embroidered imperial crown; the pearls were made of silver on an aurora background.

The crossed cannon were embroidered with light burnt Sienna wool and were surrounded with a little gold cord; as for the leaves, they were embroidered plain; their stalks, tassels, grains and leaves and nervures were made of gold cord; the lightning strokes and the pennons were red. As with the troopers' sabretaches, the NCOs' were given the metal eagle in 1811.

The base of the cartridge case was made of browned brass.

THE TRUMPETERS

When it was created, the Horse Artillery Company of the Consular Guard had two trumpeters, then four by the end of the year.

A Brigadier-trumpeter joined them at the beginning of 1802.

Two new trumpeters joined the corps when the second company was formed at the end of 1802. When the Horse Artillery of the Imperial Guard – with three two-company squadrons – its strength grew to 18, commanded by a trumpet-major and a brigadier trumpeter.

(continued on page 105)

NCOs from light Artillery

NCO wearing full parade dress, according to L. Rousselot. Note the shape of the stripes worn by the NCOs.

NCO wearing campaign dress, according to L. Rousselot

Maréchal des Logis-chef wearing a frock coat, according to L. Rousselot.

NCO wearing campaign dress in 1806, according to a painting by A. Vafflard, to be found in the Musée de Versailles.

Trumpeter wearing full parade dress

Trumpeter wearing full parade dress in 1812, according to Vallet in the Noirmont and Marbot Collection.

Sabretache at the end of the Empire.

Trumpeter wearing full parade dress in 1807 after plate N° 74 by L. Rousselot.

Trumpeter wearing full parade dress in 1812, according to Knötel. Although dated from the end of the Empire, L. Rousselot thinks it's more likely to be from the beginning of the Empire. In the same way, apparently, there was only one single saddlecloth, shown opposite.

Trumpeter wearing full parade dress in 1807 after plate N° 74 by L. Rousselot.

Trumpeter wearing full parade dress

Trumpeter wearing marching dress, according to a watercolour by L. Rousselot. In theory, the white colback was kept for the full-dress uniform. This practice was encountered however mainly at the end of the Empire.

Trumpeter wearing campaign dress in about 1813-1814, according to a watercolour by L. Rousselot. The leather sabretache replaced the fragile embroidered sabretache.
The cartridge case was the NCO's model.

Trumpeter wearing an à la chasseur coat, in about 1807, according to a water colour by L. Rousselot.
The coat bears the gold stripe of the function.
The waistcoat is decorated with mixed crimson and gold cord.

The Trumpeters

Trumpeter wearing service dress.

Trumpeter wearing campaign dress in about 1807.

Trumpeter wearing town dress.

Trumpeter wearing town dress with cloak dress.

Waistcoat.

A la chasseur coat.

Trumpeter wearing campaign dress in about 1813, according to drawing by JOB. The source is a painting of the same period as Lassus. The uniform can be justified by a lack of specific trumpeter items

The Officers

Officer wearing a tail coat, according to A. Martinet.

A la chasseur coat.

Officer wearing a tail coat, according to L. Rousselot in his plate N° 74.

Officer wearing a tail coat, according to a portrait in the old Franck Collection.

Officer wearing campaign dress during the Prussian Campaign, according to L. Rousselot.

The Officers

Type 1804 standard, obverse and reverse sides.

Crowned eagle at the time of the return from the Polish Campaign, 25 November 1807. The standard was given a crown at the Barrière de la Villette by the City of Paris.

Crowned eagle

Officer wearing full parade dress (mounted).

Officer wearing full parade dress.

Officer wearing summer service dress, according to L. Rousselot in his plate N° 74.

Cartridge pouch. There are other variants, displayed in the various museum collections.

(continued from page 98)

In 1808, the regiment was reduced to two squadrons and the trumpeters were the only eight under the command of a trumpet-major. From 1813 to the first abdication, there were 12 trumpeters with a trumpet-major. In 1815 when they were reformed, the number of trumpeters rose to 12, plus a trumpet-major and a brigadier trumpeter with 12 trumpeters.

The trumpeters' uniform

When the company was created, it is most likely that, as with the other trumpeters in the cavalry units of the Consular Guard, the dress was sky blue. The colbacks were blue and their cord, like the trimmings, was a mix of gold and wool. The grenades on the turnbacks were gold.

Like the troopers, the trumpeters had two uniforms, one à la hussarde and the other à la chasseur - both of which were made of sky blue cloth with crimson distinctives.

The colback was worn with the full uniform; another, black, one was worn with the undress uniform. As well as the body made of fur, these two headpieces were made up of *"leather chinstraps covered with a little brass chain, a tricolour cockade and sky-blue pennon decorated with little cords and a gold and crimson tassel"*[5].

A cord ending with flounders and tassels formed a plait on the front of the headpiece. A little later in the period, the cord became a simple strand. Tassels, flounders and cords were mixed gold and crimson in the same proportions as the rest of the trimmings.

The full-dress plume was probably sky blue with a white summit; the one worn in other circumstances was scarlet, even if in certain circumstances the full-dress plume seems to have taken its place on the top of the undress uniform colback.

After 1811, the undress uniforms of the Artillery were fitted with a crimson flame whereas the white furred colback retained its sky-blue flame.

The bicorn (hat)

The hat was worn mainly with town dress and was decorated with crimson and gold cord loops, the classic gold cockade cord. The ornamental ovals in the corners were crimson with a gold centre. The scarlet undress uniform plume was added to this.

The dolman

The trumpeters like the gunners received at first the à la hussarde dress without the pelisse. The dolman was made of crimson cloth with sky-blue facings and collars. It and its decoration were fastened by five rows of yellow buttons. The flat tress, the square cord and the Russian braid were mixed one third gold and two thirds sky blue. The dolman remained crimson and the pelisse sky blue until the end of the Empire.

The pelisse

In 1801, the trumpeters received a crimson pelisse edged with black sheep skin. Its buttons, flat tress, square tress and Russian braid were the same as on the dolman. The hanging cord and its olive were mixed gold and sky blue. In 1806, the sky-blue pelisse was decorated with gold and crimson trimmings.

The pink of the dolman and the pelisse, or a sky-blue dolman were mistakes popularised by the work of a host of illustrators in the second half of the 19th century. This à la hussarde uniform did not change until the end of the Empire.

The *à la chasseur* coat

The à la chasseur uniform was made up of the coat, braided - or plain - waistcoat, the Hungarian breeches or riding breeches.

This coat was made of sky-blue cloth, the turnbacks and the lining of the skirts were the same colour; the collar, the pointed lapels and the facings, also pointed were dark blue edged with crimson; the same border edged the turnbacks and the fold flaps.

The collar was given gold braid, like the lapels and the facings. This border formed a decoration on the waist. The turnbacks were decorated with gold embroidered grenades and the shoulder loops were gold braid. The aglet placed on the left-hand side was mixed one third gold and two thirds crimson wool.

The braided trefoil was mounted on crimson cloth on the right-hand side. The coat was worn according to the instructions with the sky blue or plain waistcoat.

At the beginning of 1812, the trumpeters in the artillery train received the same uniforms as those distributed to the trumpeters in the Horse Artillery. The colbacks were made of bearskin decorated with a crimson flame.

The waistcoats

Like the gunner, the trumpeter had a sky-blue waistcoat with five rows of little buttons and gold and crimson trimmings, and a plain double-breasted waistcoat, crimson with two rows of buttons.

The other items of clothing

The tangled belt with cords was sky blue; its loops, knots, olive and tassels were gold mixed with crimson trimmings.

The Hungarian breeches were sky blue. The breeches with flat tresses and Hungarian knots were gold and crimson. The riding breeches were sky blue, with leather padding between the legs. A crimson coloured stripe was sewn on either side; it was decorated with 18 yellow buttons.

The black Light Cavalry boots were edged with Russian braid cut out in the form of a heart and had mixed gold and crimson tassels.

The forage cap, the stable jacket and the greatcoat-cloak were at first identical to those of the gunners; they became sky blue in around 1806-1807. The way they were worn did not change.

The trumpeters, like the gunners, once again, lost their *à la hussarde* uniform during the First Restoration and went off into Belgium wearing the à la chasseur coat.

The sabretache

The gold braided sabretache had a sky-blue background. Although at first it bore a yellow grenade

(continued on page 108)

5. *In* Lucien Rousselot *in « Les uniformes de l'armée française ».*

The Officers

Squadron commander wearing town dress, according to the Musée de l'Emperi collections.

Officer wearing service dress after a drawing by JOB, according to a period painting by Lassus. Note the sabretache without an eagle.

Officer wearing a greatcoat, according to a drawing by JOB, after a period picture by Lassus.

Officer wearing campaign dress, according to an aquarelle by L. Rousselot.

Officer wearing social dress, according to an aquarelle by L. Rousselot.

Officer wearing a tail coat, according to Weiland.

Officer wearing a tail coat, according to H. Boisselier

Senior Officers

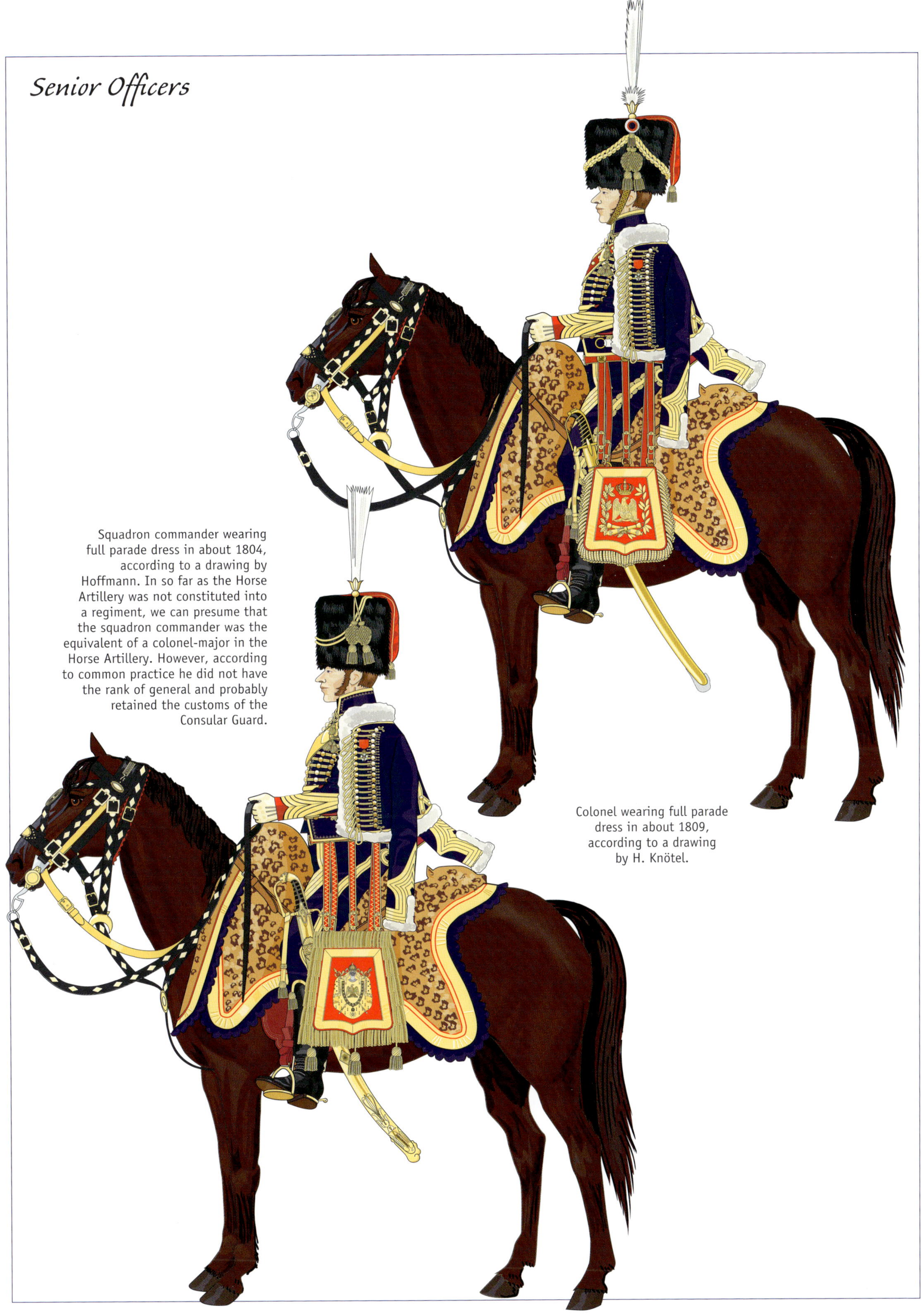

Squadron commander wearing full parade dress in about 1804, according to a drawing by Hoffmann. In so far as the Horse Artillery was not constituted into a regiment, we can presume that the squadron commander was the equivalent of a colonel-major in the Horse Artillery. However, according to common practice he did not have the rank of general and probably retained the customs of the Consular Guard.

Colonel wearing full parade dress in about 1809, according to a drawing by H. Knötel.

(continued from page 105)
surrounded by plain embroidered leaves, this was replaced with the same motif as for the troopers when the Empire began: a crowned eagle surmounting two crossed cannon.

During the Consulate, a white streamer bearing the inscription "Garde des Consuls" surmounted the grenade. In 1811, the brass eagle replaced the embroidered emblem.

Other articles of equipment

The leatherwork was like the troopers', i.e. made of white buffalo hide stitched along the edges. The cartridge case was that of the NCOs with sides made of copper and its flap was modified in the same way. In 1811, as for the troopers, the buffalo hide sabre-knot, but this time with a gold and crimson tassel, replaced the old braid and crimson knot.

The trumpeters were armed like the gunners.

The harnesses

The schabrack of the undress uniform was made of sky-blue cloth edged with scarlet piping and braid. The edges were first of all decorated with a red grenade before being replaced by a scarlet eagle.

For the Consular period, Hoffmann evoked a full-dress sky-blue schabrack, with crimson piping and decorated with gold grenades in the corners. Gold braid and its string of rings on the inside made up the decoration.

A tassel hung at each corner of the schabrack. The portmanteau was sky blue with scarlet braid and piping.

The trumpeters and the apron

The trumpeters' instrument was made of copper, and those of the trumpet-majors were silver coloured. A cord with its tassels: the one for full dress was made of gold and crimson wool, and for the undress uniform it was made of yellow and crimson wool.

An apron was added for the parades. *"During the Consulate, it was in the form of a guidon with rounded half points, made of crimson Damascene, embroidered with gold and silver with a fringe made of gold twists, little and large gold tassels and a red and gold trumpet cord."*[6]

An undress uniform pavilion should have had fringes and it would have had red and gold tassels. No source mentions the presence of the arms of the Empire on the full dress and undress aprons, even if logic would require them to do so.

THE OFFICERS OF THE HORSE ARTILLERY

The officers of the Horse Artillery of the Guard used the same items as the troopers but, of course, tailored in finer cloth and garnished with gold buttons and trimmings.

The colback

The colback used at the start of the company was low and narrow before increasing in size after 1801. The gold cord was arranged in two plaits placed on the front, one of the plaits going around the headpiece during the period.

The flounders ending with a tassel hung to the right of the headpiece, then to the left under the plume, after 1802.

The colback pennant was scarlet and its cords, like the tassel at the end, were also gold. The plume was scarlet.

The hat and the forage cap

The hat was worn for town dress had all its trimmings in gold (cockade cord, cords, loose twists). The forage cap had gold trimmings.

The dolman and the pelisse

These were decorated with five rows of buttons and were distinguished by the marks of rank, flat tresses and gold Russian braid. As soon as the corps was created, the officers – at the beginning there were four of them – wore a blue pelisse edged with grey fur.

The pelisses belonging to the senior officers had narrow stripes bordering the one already on the back seams. This layout, also to be seen on the dolman, enabled the senior officers to be identified.

After 1806, the luxury of the ornamentation on the à la hussarde clothes gradually diminished.

The coat

The coat of the undress uniform was identical in shape, colour and cut to the same pattern as that of the gunners'. The difference lay in the gold buttons, the shoulder loops and the gold turnback grenades

The coat bore the rank epaulette on the left-hand shoulder and the gold aglets on the right. The escutcheon on the shoulder bore a gold embroidered grenade.

The officers wore a braided waistcoat, Hungarian breeches and boots with the breeches for the undress uniform or, the white nankeen waistcoat, white breeches – sometimes blue – white, blue or black stockings and silver buckled shoes for town or social dress.

The waistcoat, the belt and the greatcoat

The dark blue waistcoat also had five rows of buttons. It was bordered by a flat tress and "a large quantity of Russian braid formed the buttonholes with the tress".

The sash belt worn on the dolman was made up of a red tangle and its loops, cord, stop knots, tassels and olive were all gold. The frock coat was the same as that of the NCOs; the officers had a blue greatcoat-cloak as well.

The breeches and the riding breeches

The Hungarian breeches were blue and had side seams covered with a flat tress.

The fly openings were surrounded by braid corresponding to the ranks, placed like an upturned spade.

The tress on the sides and the braid on the outside of the fly were surrounded by extremely complex Russian braid, no matter what the rank.

The campaign trousers or riding breeches were garnished with skin or cloth. It was buttoned, so-
(continued on page 114)

6. *In* Lucien Rousselot *in « Les uniformes de l'armée française ».*

The general Desvaux de Saint Maurice

Desvaux de Saint Maurice Born in Paris on 26 June 1775, Desvaus de Saint Maurice entered the Collège de Juilly as a pupil, then as a sous-lieutenant in the artillery school at Châlons on 1 March 1792. On 1 September he as an artillery lieutenant in the 4th Foot Artillery Regiment. He was promoted to First Lieutenant, and Adjudant-Major on 31 July 1793. He was assigned to the Army of the Alps under Kellermann and distinguished himself during the fighting at Aiguebelle and Saint-Maurice, then at the siege of Lyon. On 22 September 1793, he was promoted to captain and took part in the first Battle of le Boulou (14-15 October 1793).

He was the employed in the Army of the Pyrénées Orientales (An II and An III) then in the Army of England. In 1798, he as in the Army of Italy and on 23 April 1799, he was appointed Squadron Commander in the 2nd Horse Artillery. He then went in to the Reserve Army on 28 November 1800, and assigned to the 8th Horse Artillery Regiment, then to the 5th on 21 January 1802. He was made a major on 23 May 1803, then colonel in the 6th Horse Artillery on 29 October 1803. A Member of the Légion d'Honneur on 11 December 1803. On 25 January 1804, he was made aide de camp to General de Marmont. Officer of the Légion d'Honneur on 14 June 1804, he was assigned to the 1st Foot Artillery Regiment on 2 March 1805.

The coat of arms of general Desvaux de Saint Maurice.

In An XII and An XIII, he was employed in Holland then in the Grande Armée. Appointed head of the artillery in Dalmatia in 11 August 1806. In 1809 he fought at Raab and at Wagram where he took part in destroying the Austrian redoubts. Appointed colonel-major of the Horse Artillery Regiment of the Imperial Guard and Brigadier-General on 9 July 1809, he was employed at the headquarters staff of the Duke of Raguse and became Baron of the Empire on 30 October 1810.

In 1812-1813, he took part in the Russian Campaign and, at the head of the whole artillery, he destroyed the Russian redoubt at Borodino. He was promoted to Major-General on 6 November 1813. Put on the non-active list on 1 November 1814, he was made a Chevalier of the Order of Saint-Louis in 1814.

During the Hundred Days, he rallied the Emperor and was made the commander of the Artillery of the Guard on 11 April 1815. During the Battle of Waterloo, he was killed by a cannonball at the head of the battery which the Emperor had just visited.

The Horse Artillery Standard

1812-type Horse Artillery standard, common to all mounted troops of the Guard. The Emperor ordered the names of battles to be seen onto the standard, and as well as the capitals which Napoleon entered as victor. The standard was received by the regiment at the ceremony on the Champ de Mai on 1 June 1815 during the Hundred Days. This standard is today preserved in the Musée de l'Armée in Paris.

Eagle-bearer officer in 1815. The uniform during the Hundred Days boiled down to an à la chasseur coat.

Officers
Rom horse artillery in 1813, according to Lassus.
(Engraving by JOB, Private collection Rights Reserved)

Trumpeter and sous-adjudant major from the light artillery in 1813, according to Lassus.
(Engraving by JOB, Private collection Rights Reserved)

the 8-pounder

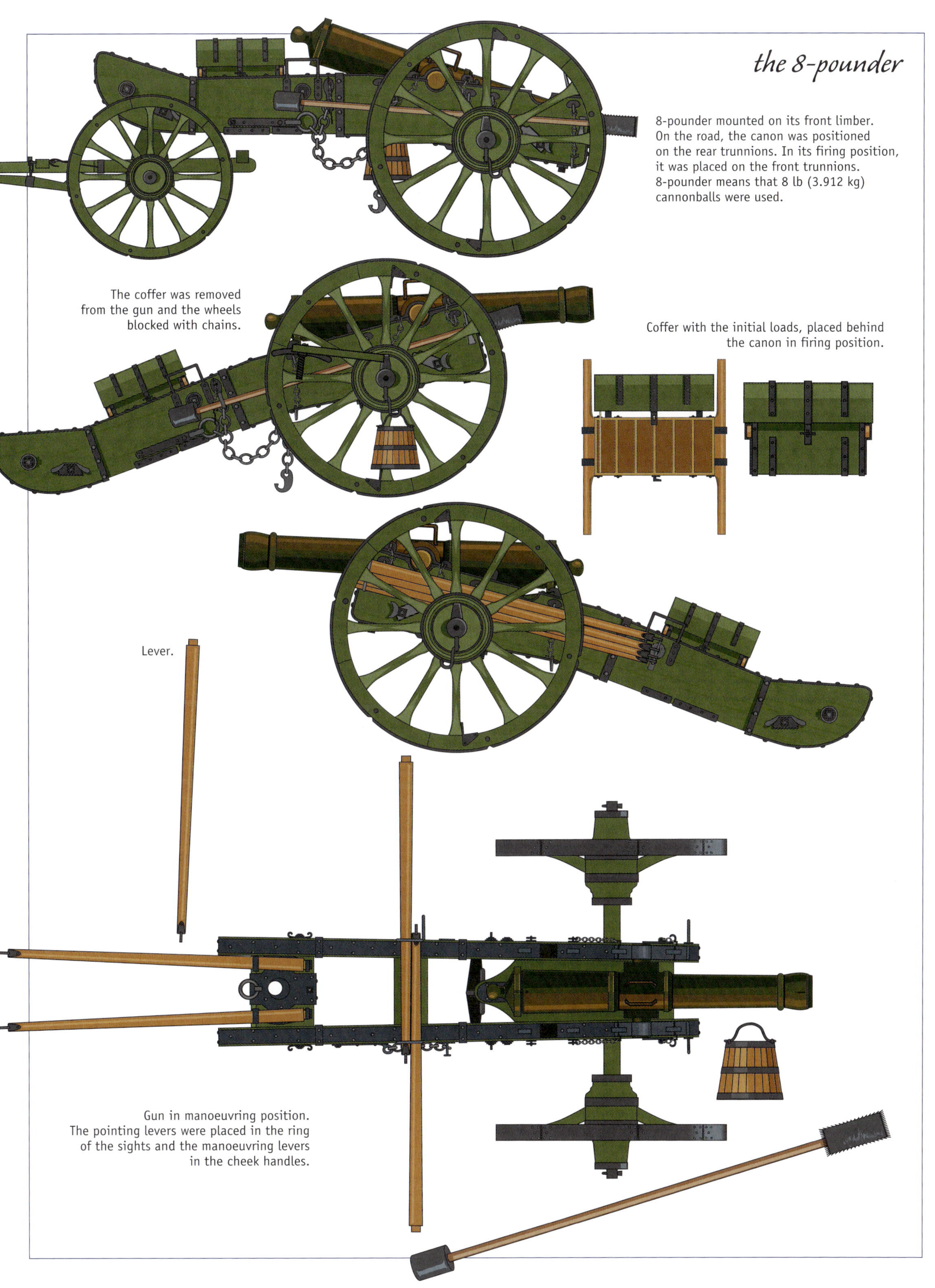

8-pounder mounted on its front limber. On the road, the canon was positioned on the rear trunnions. In its firing position, it was placed on the front trunnions. 8-pounder means that 8 lb (3.912 kg) cannonballs were used.

The coffer was removed from the gun and the wheels blocked with chains.

Coffer with the initial loads, placed behind the canon in firing position.

Lever.

Gun in manoeuvring position. The pointing levers were placed in the ring of the sights and the manoeuvring levers in the cheek handles.

Setting up an 8-pounder, in about 1807

(continued from page 108)
metimes not, on the sides and decorated with a red stripe with buttonholes or a double gold tress *(see page 104)*.

The sabretache

The background of the officers' sabretache had clearly always been scarlet edged with braid and gold Russian braid.

During the Consulate, in the centre of the plateau decorated with a grenade, gold leaves were surmounted by a streamer made of "silver cloth" where there was the caption "Garde des Consuls". During the Empire, there were a crowned eagle and two crossed cannon surrounded by oak and laurel leaves embroidered in gold.

The equipment

The equipment was made of red leather. The cartridge case strap was braided and decorated with gold attributes: lion's head, little chains, escutcheon stamped with an eagle, alone or surmounting two cannon saltire-wise. The flap of the cartridge case was cut out and edged with cane. It too was given a grenade at first then an eagle over its two cannon. The belt, the straps and the sabretache straps were edged with a gold strip. The belt rosettes and the studs covering the belt rings had "lion's heads".

Armament

The Horse Artillery officers were armed with a sabre, a sword and two tree pistols. First of all, during the Consulate, the sabre was the Light Cavalry officer's

model, or a German-style sabre (a guard with a single branch forming a right-angled cross) with a leather scabbard with more or less decorations. Later on in the period, the artillery officers used the sabre of an officer in the Chasseurs à Cheval of the Guard for parades. When campaigning, the artillery officers preferred the An-IX model sabre of the Light Cavalry officer with a three-branched guard and a metal scabbard.

The shape and decoration of the sword varied and was not specific to any particular uniform. The braid or gold cord sabre-knot ended in a fringed tassel in a line or twisted, according to the rank.

The harnessing

The parade harness comprised a panther skin schabrack placed on the panelled Hungarian saddle. It was braided with gold and edged with scarlet festoons which were subsequently blue. There was red edging around the gold braid.

The parade bridle and the halter were decorated with appliqués, nails or gold studs; the buckles and their loops, and the bit studs were also golden. A more robust and less costly harness was kept for ordinary service ever since the Consular period; blue cloth schabrack braided with gold and piped with scarlet.

The crowned eagle can be seen on certain schabracks whereas other officers kept the embroidered gold grenades.

The schabrack could be covered with a panther skin seat. The cylindrical portmanteau had ends edged with scarlet and braided with gold.

Artillery Train

Driver wearing full dress in about 1804-1806 after L. Rousselot.

Driver in Spain in about 1808, according to Gunner Hahlo's manuscript.

Driver in about 1809, according to the Berka Manuscript. This uniform resembles that of the first artillery wagon-drivers.

Driver in about 1803-1804, according to Plate N° 80 by L. Rousselot. In the artillery train, he was the front bearer.

Driver in about 1803-1804 wearing full dress.

The Artillery Train

The recently militarised artillery train entered the Consular Guard as the Light Artillery.

As far as numbers were concerned it followed the Artillery in the Guard, especially with the creation of the Foot Artillery and the great reorganisation of 1813.

Like the Gribeauval materiel, there was no particular technological improvement; on the other hand, the experience gained over twenty years of campaigning made the use of artillery evolve.

Created in 1800, the artillery train continued as a matter of course into the Consular Guard and then the Imperial Guard in 1804.

Its strength grew in line with that of the Artillery of the Guard from a six-company battalion in 1806 to two: a war battalion and a depot battalion. In 1809 the two battalions were increased by three companies to a total of 15 companies.

In 1813, the Train formed a regiment of three 4-company battalions, immediately increased by a Fourth Battalion to form two regiments in 1814 for a total of 24 companies.

During the Hundred Days, the Artillery Train was reformed as a squadron of nine companies of which one was Young Guard.

The Uniform

In fifteen years' existence, the uniforms of the Artillery Train drivers of the Guard went through a great number of changes.

The hat

At the beginning of the empire, the drivers of the Train wore a bicorn hat with a tricolour cockade and a white cord. This hat was decorated with a carrot-shaped pompom or a scarlet plume as early as 1802. Certain period representations show it even decorated with eight white loops and loose twists the same colour in the corners.

The shako

Most likely adopted in about 1808, the shako became the artillery train headpiece. It had a flounder cord and a scarlet plume or a pompom, the upper braid in the form of a dice was also scarlet. It was decorated with a plate with a base of two crossed cannon made of yellow copper.

It was in around 1809 that the rosettes on the chinstraps were replaced by crowns.

In 1812, the body of the shako was covered with iron grey cloth with the same decorations as before.

On campaign, the shako's plume and the flounder cord were removed and covered with a shako cover made of black waxed cloth.

At the end of the Empire, the shakos no longer had their flounder cord, the plume was replaced by a pompom; we do not know if the Second Regiment received shakos after the 1812 regulations.

However, in the Musée de l'Armée collections, there exists an Empire-style hat which has been attributed to the Artillery Train.

The forage cap

The forage cap with the knot was iron grey and had braid, cords, scarlet grenade and tassels.

The *habit-veste*

"When the Artillery Train of the Consular Guard was formed in September 1800, the company retained, if not the uniform, at least the colours of the former artillery waggoners, i.e. the iron grey *habit-veste* with dark blue decorations". 1

The *habit-veste* worn during the Consular period buttoned down to the belt and had small pointed lapels. It is probable that the shoulder flaps and the turnbacks were the same colour.

The collar, the lapels, the pointed facings, the edges of the three-pointed vertical pockets, and those on the shoulder flaps and the turnbacks like the grenades were dark blue.

The buttons made of tin, were stamped with the caption "Garde des Consuls". This *habit-veste* was much too dull for the men belonging to an elite unit and was quickly enhanced in 1802 with scarlet piping on the collar, the lapels, the facings, pockets and turnbacks.

The shoulder flaps were dark blue edged with red but in 1805, the full-dress uniform replaced its shoulder flaps by trefoils. Still in 1805, a *habit-veste*, cut from inferior quality cloth was used for ordinary service. It kept the shoulder flaps edged with red until 1806.

The grenades on the turnbacks became red on both models of *habit-veste* in 1806. In 1807, the *habit-veste* had iron-grey turnbacks and were edged with red, like the grenades which were sewn onto it.

The trefoils described in 1805 were present. 24 medium sized buttons were laid on this item of clothing. The three-pointed vertical pockets were replaced by à la Soubise flaps with two buttons.

In 1809, the driver's definitive look was set and the *habit-veste* only underwent minor changes. The fringed epaulettes, symbols of the elite troops, were probably worn by the Foot Artillery piece drivers; the trefoils were therefore logically reserved for the drivers of the Horse Artillery batteries.

In 1811, a new *habit-veste* was issued to the drivers. The coat was now buttoned straight down as for the Line Train and hid the waistcoat.

One à la Soubise flap was sewn onto the fold of the skirts. Its cut resembled that of the à la Kinski coat of the Chasseurs à cheval. The Guards' colours were retained.

The waistcoats

During the Consulate, there was a variety of cuts and colours of waistcoats.

On the painting by Lejeune of the Battle of Marengo, a driver of African origin was wearing "a yellow waistcoat and a loose red cravat."[2] In 1802 an iron grey waistcoat was adopted. A white waistcoat was adopted for the full-dress uniform at the beginning of 1805.

In 1809, a braided waistcoat decorated with three rows of 15 little tin buttons was issued to the drivers and confirmed in 1811.

(continued on page 119)

1. *In* Lucien Rousselot *in « Les uniformes de l'armée française ».*

2. *Ibid.*

The Drivers

Driver in about 1807-1810 wearing full dress; he is the rear bearer. In the Guard, the driver sat on a dragoon's saddle, shown here without its portmanteau.
Driver in about 1807-1810 wearing full dress.
Sabre belt.
Cartridge pouch.
Small sabre.
Artillery driver's coat in 1810.
Driver in about 1807-1810 wearing full dress, rear view.
For practical reasons, the sabre belt was worn over the shoulder, saltire-wise.
Driver in about 1807-1810 wearing full dress, Left view.

The greatcoat-cloak

The drivers' wardrobe also included a double-breasted greatcoat-cloak with a rotunda cape.

The breeches

At first the drivers had Hungarian breeches made of sheepskin then, in 1809, they were issued with iron grey à la hussarde cloth breeches with scarlet braid.

The over-trousers or riding breeches

These were iron grey, padded with black calfskin between the legs, and closed on the side. There was a red band with buttons. In 1813, grey riding trousers were issued padded with skins.

The boots

The boots were *à la Russe*, i.e. stiff, with boot sleeves made of skin in order to protect the sheepskin breeches from rubbing on the leather. The spurs were cavalry-style. In 1809, the drivers received à la hussarde boots and their blackened iron spurs were attached *in situ*. In 1813, the drivers were issued with *à l'écuyère* boots, but this time the American model and their removable cavalry-style spurs with their mounts.

Stable dress

The iron grey stable jacket, including the collar, fastened by means of a row of 18 buttons in the front and four on the waist braid. Plain iron grey cloth trousers, buttoned on the side, made up the ensemble. The artillery train drivers also had strong deerskin gloves.

After the Russian Campaign

For ordinary dress, the train used the iron-grey cloth coat buttoning straight down in front with dark blue collar and turnbacks and scarlet piping. This second uniform coat decorated with trefoils or epaulettes was worn with the skin breeches and the stiff boots which were more suitable for driving a train.

In 1813, both regiments wore the iron grey *habit-veste* with dark blue lapels, collar, turnbacks decorated with scarlet piping in the First Regiment and iron grey in the 2nd. It was also the return to the skin breeches and the cavalry boots for full dress and the cavalry breeches made of iron grey cloth with the same boots in campaign dress.

The uniform of the Second Regiment

The Second Regiment of the Artillery Train of the Guard was formed in April 1813; its uniform was that of the Line. Its iron grey and dark blue *habit-veste* had shoulder flaps; its shako had neither cord nor plume, the visor was not circled and the chinstrap rosettes bore a star; finally, it was decorated with a tassel.

During the Hundred Days, the squadron of the Artillery Train was issued with a uniform inspired by the one worn in 1811.

It comprised a so-called "Polish" stable jacket with short skirts, decorated with red fringed epaulettes, iron grey Hungarian breeches, *à l'écuyère* boots with removable spurs. The shako no longer had a cord but retained the red plume.

The Gribeauval System 8-pounder gun was hitched up to, and drawn by, a double team, with four horses: two carrier horses (on the left) and two off-horses (on the right); the two rear horses were hitched up on either side of the wagon pole of the front limber. As well as their job of pulling and steadying, they steered the front limber. The two front horses were hitched up to the end of the wagon pole by a swingle-tree linked to its holders.

Note that for transportation, the gun was placed on the rear position of the gun carriage and held in place.

The bucket was hung underneath the gun carriage. On uneven terrain, it was possible to hitch up two further horses.

Equipment

First of all, without a visible plate, the baldric was the infantry model. It was then stitched and garnished with a gudgeon in the form of a sword and bayonet holder, with a ring, hooks and brown copper buttons.

The plate on the white and stitched buffalo hide belt was stamped with a grenade. A cartridge pouch belt appeared in 1809, when the soldier's cartridge pouch of the model of the Artillery of the Guard was adopted.

Armament

First of all, the driver was armed with a short sabre with a knot made of white buffalo hide. In April 1809 a pistol was issued to each soldier. A holster was placed on the left-hand side of every saddle but nothing was done to cover it.

The portmanteau

Each soldier in the Train was issued with an iron grey portmanteau, with white braid like in the Line, then scarlet in 1811. In 1809, a cylindrical iron-grey portmanteau was adopted when the à la hussarde breeches were handed out.

Harnessing

The *à la dragonne* saddles of the bearer horses remained plain until the Second Abdication. An iron grey half-saddlecloth braided with white and the white sheepskin half-schabrack edged with iron grey. There is no precise description of the harnesses for the draught horses.

The NCOs

The NCOs had a uniform which was quite different from that of the troopers. Indeed, even if iron grey was common, the coat had long skirts with lapels and pointed facings.

The waistcoat was iron grey and braided as early as the Consulate. The NCOs wore Hungarian breeches and à la hussarde boots.

The NCOs' headpieces

Their hats had a silver cockade cord and a red plume. The trimmings of their uniforms were two thirds scarlet to one third silver: aglet mounted on a trefoil and worn on the left; trefoil on the right-

(continued on page 124)

The Drivers

Driver in the First Regiment in about 1813-1814, after a plate by L. Rousselot.

Driver wearing marching dress during the Russian Campaign.

Driver wearing stable dress.

Driver in about 1810-1811, according to the set of plates by Noirmont and Marbot.

Driver wearing marching dress.

The Drivers about 1813

Artillery driver wearing campaign dress in 1813.

Artillery driver wearing full dress in about 1813.

Driver from the First Regiment, wearing full dress in about 1813-1814.

This dress has been reconstituted from a coat and a hat preserved in the Musée de l'Armée in Paris.

Driver in about 1815, after L. Rousselot.

Driver, First Class, in about 1812-1813.

Driver in about 1813, in the Dresden Camp.

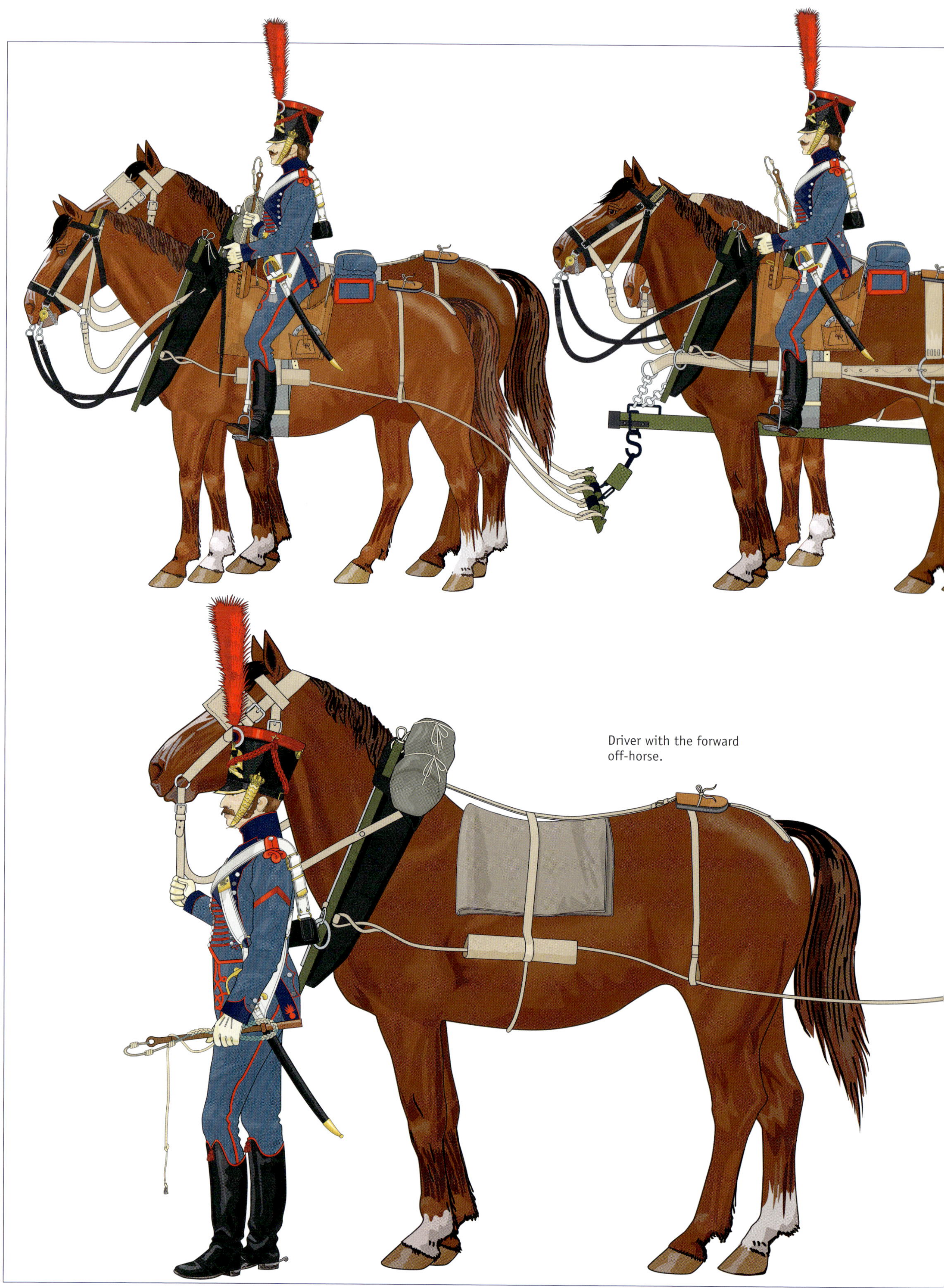

Driver with the forward off-horse.

The hitched up 8-pounder

The Gribeauval System 8-pounder gun was hitched up to, and drawn by, a double team, with four horses: two carrier horses (on the left) and two off-horses (on the right); the two rear horses were hitched up on either side of the wagon pole of the front limber. As well as their job of pulling and steadying, they steered the front limber. The two front horses were hitched up to the end of the wagon pole by a swingle-tree linked to its holders.
Note that for transportation, the gun was placed on the rear position of the gun carriage and held in place. The bucket was hung underneath the gun carriage. On uneven terrain, it was possible to hitch up two further horses.

Driver with the rear off-horse.

(continued from the page 119)
hand shoulder; flat tress and Russian braid on the waistcoat.

Until 1812, the colback was the service headdress for NCOs. The NCOs' hat had decorations, probably silver and the red ovals with a silver centre were placed in the corners of the bicorn hats.

In April 1809, shakos and cartridge cases were issued to the NCOs.

"This shako had a silver stripe on its upper edge and the same plates and chinstraps as that of the troopers." The plaited cord and the flounders were red, mixed with one third silver.

The coat

The à la chasseur coat was thus made of iron-grey cloth with turnbacks the same colour. The embroidered grenades were silver. The collar, the lapels and the pointed facings were imperial blue, edged with red. The turnbacks and the fold flaps were the same.

The flat tress decorating the Hungarian breeches, the decorations on the boots, the sabre-knot, the little cords and the oval ornaments on the hat were also mixed scarlet and silver.

The embroidered waistcoat was iron grey. It was garnished with five rows of little buttons of the Train.

The Hungarian breeches were decorated with a flat tress and a Hungarian knot. The iron-grey trousers, garnished with calfskin had an imperial blue stripe and silver semi-spherical buttons. As with the drivers, this dress seems to have been worn as it was until 1809.

Just like their juniors, the officers were issued
(continued on page 128)

The Gribeauval system ordinary Caisson

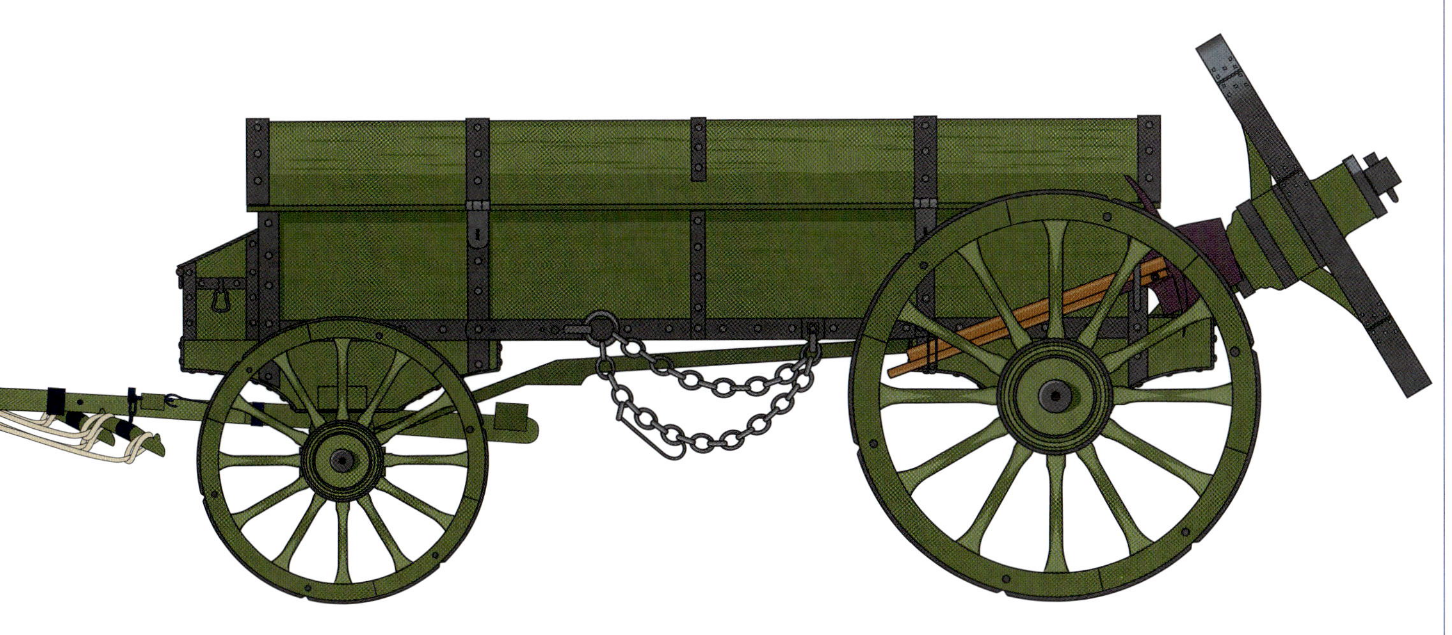

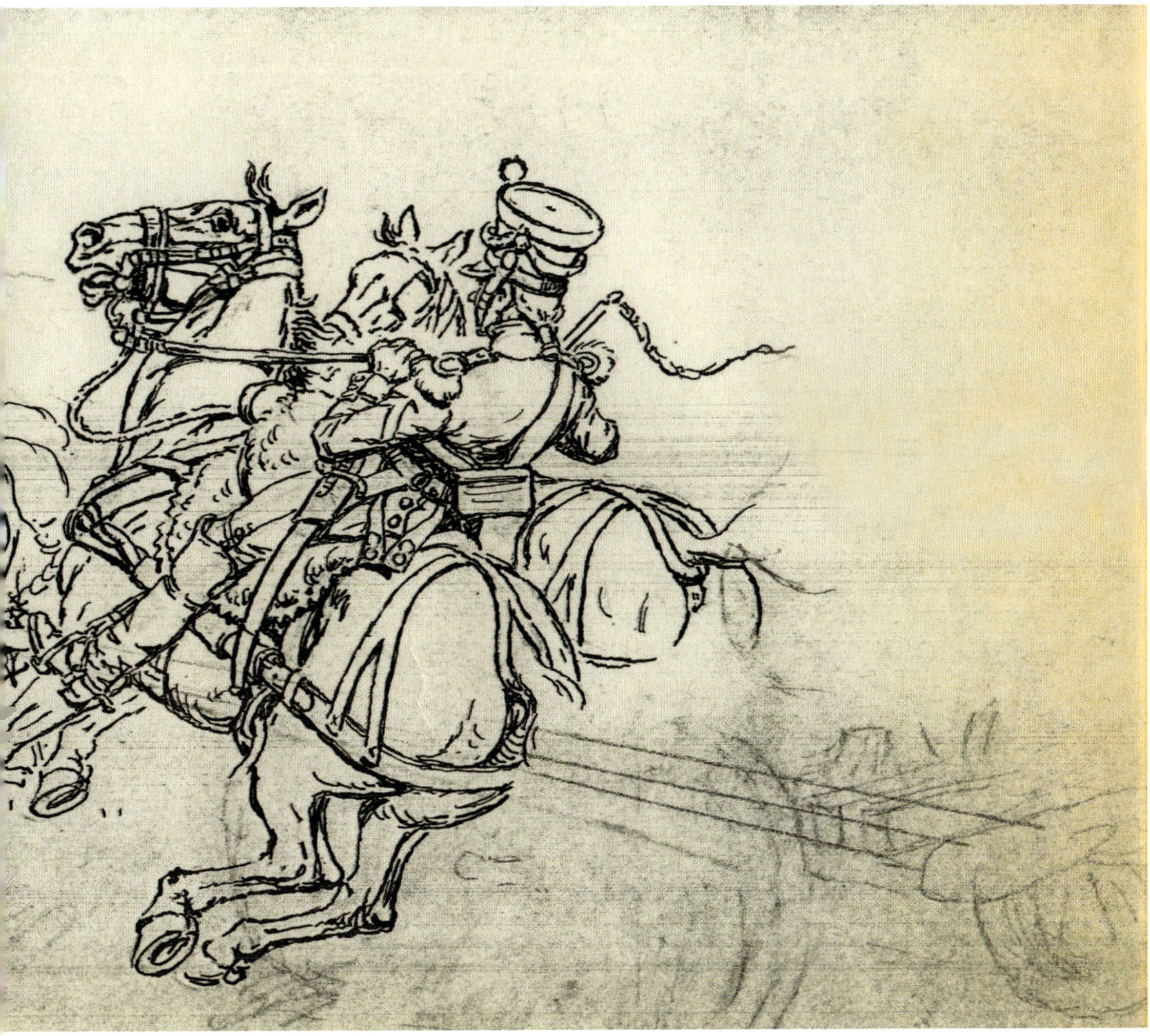

On this draft of Eugène Lelièpvre we recognize the Artillery Train of the Guard. *(Private Collection, Rights Reserved)*

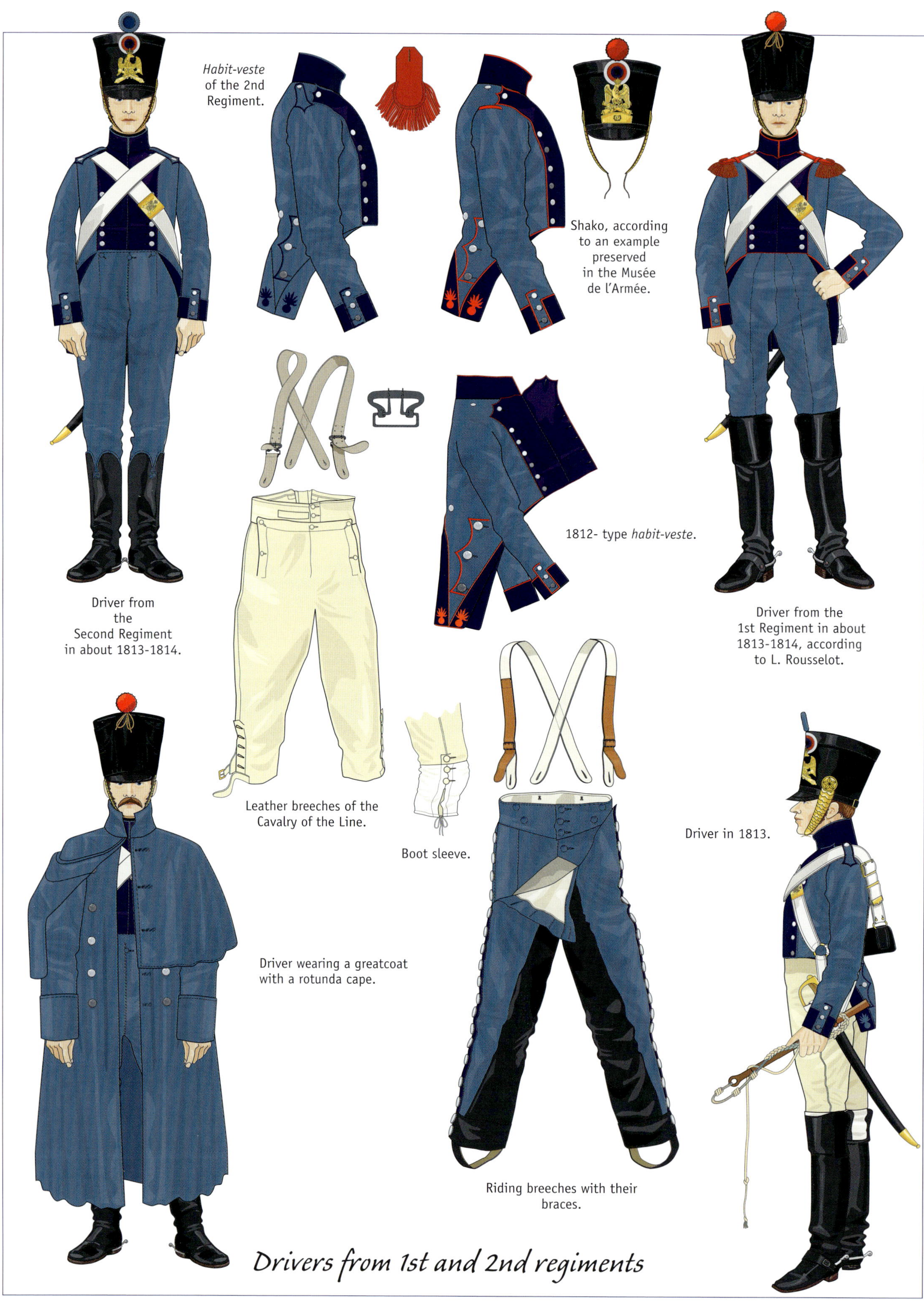

Drivers from 1st and 2nd regiments

NCOs

Maréchal des Logis in about 1804-1809 wearing marching dress, according to Plate N° 106 by L. Rousselot.

Maréchal des Logis in about 1804-1809, according to Plate N° 100 by L. Rousselot.

Brigadier in about 1804-1806, according to Plate N° 100 by L. Rousselot.

Maréchal des Logis wearing full dress in about 1811, according to Plate N° 100 by L. Rousselot.

Maréchal des Logis wearing campaign dress in 1815, according to Plate N° 100 by L. Rousselot.

The Gribeauval system ordinary Caisson and wagon

The Gribeauval Ordinary caisson.

(continued from page 124)
with plain Hungarian breeches, greatcoat-cloaks and coats for the full dress and undress uniforms.

The cartridge case like that of the Horse Artillery reserved for the officers had copper sides.

From Russia to Belgium

In 1812, the NCOs received Hungarian breeches made of sheepskin and Russian-style boots. When the square lapelled *habit-veste* was adopted the NCOs received this new item of clothing with the same rank stripes, turnback ornamentation and aglets as previously.

The NCOs' shako was made of iron-grey cloth and had its upper edge braided with silver; the plate, the chinstraps and the crowns were made of silver copper. The cord was logically made of silver and red tresses. This uniform remained the same until the end of the Empire.

When campaigning, the NCOs wore over breeches and a shako cover.

The NCOs in the Second Regiment had no other distinctions than the silver rank stripes. As with the drivers, during the Hundred Days, the NCOs wore the so-called "Polish" stable jacket.

It was more simply tailored compared with that of the troopers; not a single ounce of scarlet cloth was used to make it. The rank stripes, the aglet and the trefoil were added.

The breeches were made of iron grey cloth and the boots were *à l'écuyère*.

The brigadiers wore the same dress as the troopers with rank markings made of red wool.

The equipment, the cartridge case, the belt – or the baldric – and the armament were the same as the troopers.

The harnessing

The NCOs used the à la dragonne saddle, with the sheepskin half-schabrack on the cover. In the second part of the period, the saddle had no holsters, nor covers nor hoods.

In 1809, the Light Cavalry harnessing and the cloth schabrack, similar to that of the Horse Artillery, but with an iron-grey background with grenades in the corners, was envisaged for all ranks of NCOs.

In 1811, eagles embroidered with red wool for their schabracks were ordered.

The portmanteau was iron grey with red braid from 1812 onwards.

In 1815, despite the change of issue, the harness remained the same.

THE OFFICERS

The illustrations of officers are very rare and the uniforms they are wearing being sometimes much less beautiful than those of the NCOs, makes them suspect.

One of the rare illustrations to come down to us is the "Officer driving the guns". He is entirely clothed in dark blue and his French-style coat has serrated and square lapels. The officer is wearing a superb

The Gribeauval
Ordinary wagon to carry tools.

embroidered waistcoat, Hungarian breeches and à la hussarde boots.

The officers wore a shako with braid and silver cord, with silver metallic decorations. The embroidered waistcoat was iron grey but it could also be scarlet.

The leatherwork was black braid with silver and gold attributes. The harness was *à la hongroise* of which all the ornamentation was silver. The schabrack and portmanteau were logically iron grey with silver braid.

Nothing proves that the officers wore colbacks.

THE TRUMPETERS

There were two trumpeters in the Artillery Train in 1803, then there were four and at the end of the year there were eight.

In 1806, the corps comprised six companies with a total of twelve trumpeters.

In 1807, after a Second Battalion was created, there were therefore 24 trumpeters on the rolls. This number did not change before the First Abdication.

A brigadier-trumpeter and an extra trumpeter for the depot joined the corps in 1811. The Second Regiment, formed in 1813, also had 24 trumpeters and a brigadier.

For the Belgian Campaign, sixteen trumpeters and a brigadier trumpeter were assigned to the squadron. Two trumpeters accompanied the Young Guard Company.

The uniform

The trumpeters of the Train were first of all dressed like those of the squadron of Horse Artillery. As a result, four trumpeters' aprons made of crimson damascene were required for the full-dress uniform, embroidered with gold and silver, like the trumpeters of the artillery.

Between 1808 and 1809, the trumpeters wore the sky blue à la chasseur coat, with dark blue collar,

THE GUARD – A PSYCHOLOGICAL WEAPON

Ever since it was created, the strength of the Guard continued to increase for the duration of the duration of the Empire, increasing from 9,798 men in 1804 to 56,169 in 1812. This unit became the supreme reserve confronting the Russian threat, even if this threat appeared more or less pressing after the treaties (Tilsitt) and the meetings (Erfurt).

Unfortunately, Alexander I never disarmed. For Napoleon, his Guard was still a determining element in his 1812 invasion plans. Paradoxically, the Guard was hardly used before Moscow.

Although its feats of arms in Spain, at Austerlitz, Eylau, or Wagram rather proved its worth, the Guard was rarely engaged. Its presence on the battlefield alone was enough to produce a terrible psychological effect on the enemy's morale, whilst at the same time inspiring the other French troops. Unfortunately for the team spirit within the body of the Grande Armée – and the distinction became more and more noticeable as the years went by – the Guard remained a privileged corps benefiting from considerable advantages and this was the cause of real jealousy within the ranks of the Line regiments. The Guard was the main reserve force during the whole of the Campaign for France, at Montmirail, Vauchamps or Champaubert. On the other hand at Waterloo, its hesitations and holding back – one can even say its flight – threw the last heroes over the edge into the precipice...

The artillery train of the Imperial Guard crossing a water cut.
(Engraving by Philippoteaux, Private Collection, Rights Reserved)

Towards the *à la hussarde* dress

The black colback of the ordinary dress of the Horse Artillery trumpeters was worn until the end of 1809.

At the end of that year, shakos were issued.

These headpieces wee covered with crimson cloth and were braided with silver on their top edge (2/3 - 1/3).

The shako was decorated with a scarlet mixed with silver (2/3 - 1/3) plaited cord, a white pompom and plume.

The metal parts – the plate, the chinstraps and the visor circle – were made of brass.

It was in 1811 that the trumpeters of the Artillery Train finished their change by adopting an entirely à la hussarde uniform.

"We note blue cloth for the greatcoat-cloaks, schabracks, stable jackets, decorated trousers, waistcoats and coats, crimson cloth for the dolmans and the piping of the coats, some 22-mm gold braid for the coats, some à la hussarde buttons made of copper, à la hussarde belts, Hungarian saddles, à la hussarde *boots garnished with a little gold and wool cord, gold for the coats and gold and wool olives, sabre-knots, flat tresses, square cords and gold and wool Russian braid, strong cord and gold and wool olives for the pelisses, garnishing for the gold grenades for the coats, aglets 1/3 gold and 2/3 crimson wool with trefoils and colback cords."*

It was still in 1811 that the colbacks were given crimson coloured flame.

In 1812, the uniforms ordered before the Russian Campaign and finally received at the beginning of 1813, fixed the trumpeters' silhouette until 1814.

During the Hundred Days, as with the Horse Artillery, the *à la hussarde* uniform was abandoned.

The trumpeters went off campaigning with their old undress uniform coat with padded trousers; the plain waistcoat was sky blue; they wore a colback.

The harnessing

The horse's harness was that of the Artillery, with the schabrack and sky-blue portmanteau with scarlet braid.

The grenades were in the corners of the schabrack. During the first months of 1810, new embroidered woollen eagles were used to decorate the corners of the schabrack.

The trumpeters in the Second Regiment

The uniform of the trumpeters in the Second Regiment, created in 1813, was simplified. White wool braid edged the collar, the lapels, the facings of the troopers' *habit-veste*.

(continued from page 129)
lapels and facings edged with scarlet as well as the à la soubise flaps.

The buttons were silver, a 22-mm silver braid stripe edged the collar, the lapels and the facings and form an escutcheon with the buttons at the waist.

The embroidered grenades of the turnbacks were silver.

The embroidered waistcoat and the Hungarian breeches were sky blue and the à la hussarde boots were decorated with a little cord and a red mixed with silver tassel.

All the trimmings (aglets, trefoil, flat tress and Russian braid) were made of two thirds of red wool mixed with one third of silver.

THE GUARD, A REFLECTION OF EUROPE OF ITS TIMES

The Guard was also a mixture of the nations of Europe who were allies of the Empire.

At the time of Napoleon's marriage to Marie-Louise, Dutch, Poles, Belgians, Italians, Rhinelanders, Swiss, Armenians etc., were to be found in the Imperial Guard.

The Guard was present in the Spanish sierras, in the distant marches of Germany. Only the depot battalions were stationed within and around Paris while the war battalions covered the Empire, trudging along its roads.

The Officers
Maréchal des Logis wearing
campaign dress
in 1813-1814.
Maréchal des Logis wearing
campaign dress
in 1813-1814, according
to Plate N° 106
by L. Rousselot.
According to
a contemporary painting,
this man was a vet.
Officer in 1806,
taken from a
contemporary
engraving.
Officer in 1805,
after a contemporary
portrait taken
from the Franck
Collection.
Officer in 1809-1814,
according to Alsatian
Collections.

The Trumpeters

Trumpeter wearing campaign dress in 1815 after plate n° 106 by L. Rousselot.

Trumpeter from the Second Regiment in about 1813. The uniform is identical to that of the other soldiers except for the white stripe which shows what his job was.

The Trumpeters at the end of the Empire

Trumpeter from the Second Regiment wearing full dress in about 1809-1811, according to Plate N° 106 by L. Rousselot.

Trumpeter wearing full dress in about 1812-1814, according to Plate N° 106 by L. Rousselot. Note that this Hussar-style dress is almost identical to that of the Horse Artillery.

The Wagon Train

The wagon trains were officially created by Napoleon during the Polish Campaign. The Guard nonetheless had its own organisation: each regiment had its own wagons and drivers. The 11 August 1811 Imperial Decree created the Wagon Train which centralised all the Guard's transport. It also had to look after the supplies, the ambulances, the Engineer Corps tools and the transport of funds. Their numbers increased while preparing for the invasion of Russia and were maintained until the end of the Empire.

In the decree dated 15 April 1806 reorganising the Guard, Article 38 stipulated that each corps of the Guard would have its own wagons, drivers and draft horses which would always be on standby, ready to march at a moment's notice. The same applied to the Guard's field hospital. These wagon drivers did not form a military corps; they were waggoners attached to each regiment with their own particular uniforms. To that was added a battalion of administration workers which had its own wagon drivers, together with bakers and other trades connected with supplying food and forage. Its drivers also drove the Guards ambulance wagons.

Only after the decree dated 24 August 1811 was a Wagon Train Battalion set up to militarise transport and centralise the organisation of the wagons. The wagons were all the responsibility of the Wagon Trains and were then organised into corps. The battalion comprised headquarters and four companies increasing to six in war-time.

The first company was thus in charge of transporting clothes, money and regimental papers; the second was assigned to the Guards' medical service and was responsible for the field hospitals, the ambulance wagons and the clothes wagons. The other companies were responsible for transport without any task being assigned in particular. Moreover, a field forge harnessed and driven by Wagon Train personnel was also seconded to each cavalry regiment.

While it was getting ready to cross the Niemen in June 1811, the battalion was increased to nine companies then reorganised after the retreat from Moscow. During the Hundred Days, the Wagon Train was reorganised again into a two hundred man squadron which, in the light of events, was very quickly reinforced by an auxiliary wagon train company led by retired officers and NCOs.

(continued on page 140)

A field forge was assigned to each cavalry regiment of the Guard. It was usually drawn by a team of four horses reduced to two on suitable terrain. Apart from the forge with bellows, there was all the equipment needed to change horseshoes as near as possible to where the regiment was.

The field Forge and the Wagon Train by Eugène Lelièpvre for *Historex*.
(Private Collection, Rights Reserved)

The Field forge

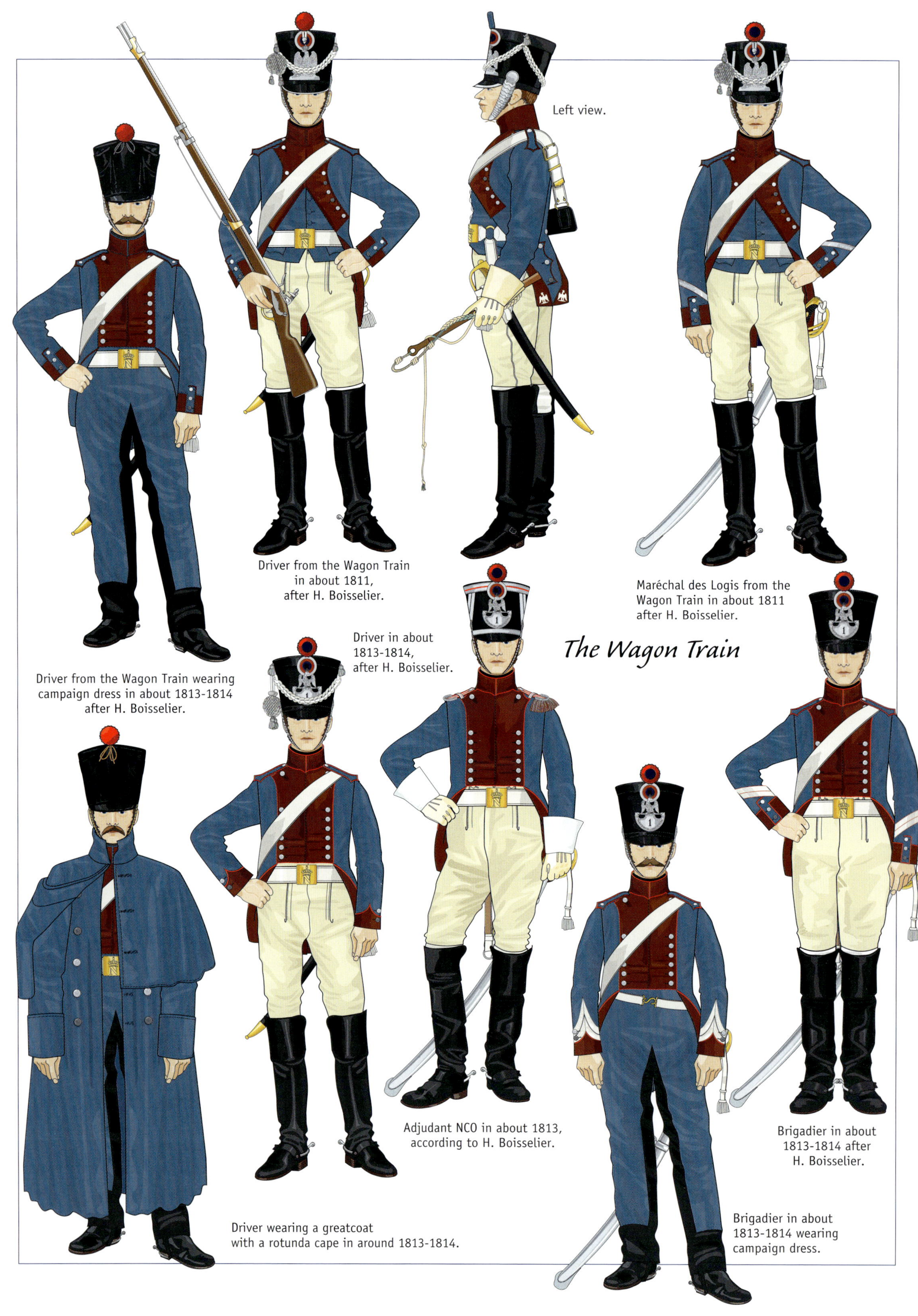

Driver from the Wagon Train in about 1811, after H. Boisselier.

Maréchal des Logis from the Wagon Train in about 1811 after H. Boisselier.

The Wagon Train

Driver in about 1813-1814, after H. Boisselier.

Driver from the Wagon Train wearing campaign dress in about 1813-1814 after H. Boisselier.

Adjudant NCO in about 1813, according to H. Boisselier.

Brigadier in about 1813-1814 after H. Boisselier.

Driver wearing a greatcoat with a rotunda cape in around 1813-1814.

Brigadier in about 1813-1814 wearing campaign dress.

Drivers from the Wagon Train

Driver from the Wagon Train in 1813, according to Commandant Bucquoy's card collections.

Officer from the Wagon Train in 1813, according to Commandant Bucquoy's card collections.

The Trumpeters

Trumpeter from the Wagon Train in 1812 after Commandant Bucquoy's card collections.

Trumpeter from the Wagon Train in 1812, according to the Alsatian Card Collections.

Trumpeter from the Wagon Train in 1813-1814, after a plate by H. Boisselier with uniform variants.

Trumpeter from the Wagon Train in 1813-1814, after a plate by H. Boisselier.

Drivers from the Wagon Train

Driver from the Administration Workers Company, according to a plate by H. Boisselier who took notes from the War Archives.

Maréchal des Logis in the Administration Workers Company, according to a plate by H. Boisselier who took notes from the War Archives.

Driver from the Wagon Train in about 1811, according to Noirmont and Marbot.

Driver from the Wagon Train in about 1811, according to Marco de St Hilaire.

Driver from the Wagon Train in about 1811 after a plate by Grammont.

The transport wagon of the Wagon Train

Transport wagon driven by the Wagon Train teams. It was normally harnessed to four horses, but could also be harnessed to two horses if it wasn't fully laden.

(continued from the page 134)

The Uniform

Before 1811, the drivers employed by the various corps were very likely clothed by the corps and the uniforms probably matched those worn by the regiments they belonged to.

On the other hand, the drivers in the administration workers battalion went around in a uniform which has already been described in Volume One of the Imperial Guard devoted to the troops on foot.

When the Guards' Wagon Trains were created the prescribed uniform was that of the Line Wagon Train. But so that they could be distinguished from the Line, the soldiers in the Guard Train wore a shako embellished with an eagle-stamped white metal plate; their turnbacks were decorated with an eagle and their buttons were the same as the Guard's. It's very likely that at the time the drivers in the worker battalion incorporated into the Wagon Train were able to keep their iron-grey uniforms and that both uniforms co-existed for a time.

This is perhaps the reason why previous authors have shown Wagon Train uniforms with the same colour distinctives and red or blue piping. After the retreat from Moscow, the cut was tailored according to the 1812 regulations with the colours and distinctives of the Train, but highlighted with red piping. The equipment was quite the same as that used by the Artillery. Althoug Service not specified, it is very likely that the drivers were armed with a pistol since they carried a cartridge pouch.

The NCOs were dressed like the other ranks but with rank markings on their sleeves and a silver stripe on the upper edge of the shako.

Trumpeters and Officers

When the battalion was created, we know of a trumpeter dressed à la Chasseur of which the background colour of the coat was brown; it was

improperly attributed to the Guards' Horse Artillery whose uniforms never used that colour. When the 1812 Regulations were put into effect, the trumpeters wore the same *habit-veste* as the other ranks, but adorned with red and gold braid whose design is still unclear.

The officers wore an iron-grey à la Chasseur coat which one supposes was paler than that of the Artillery Train, but this remains unattested. They wore a silver aglet.

The Baggage Wagon

Baggage wagon used by the Guard Wagon Train. Normally four horses teamed up, as with the artillery trains with the 8-pounders, but it is shown here with only two horses to fit the page better and make the picture clearer.

This type of wagon was used for transporting all sorts of items, all the papers and impedimenta which a regiment found indispensable. It is most likely that the majority of these wagons were painted the same colour as the artillery gun carriages, or deeper ochre, but there is no certainty about the exact colour.

The Field Forge

One field forge was assigned to each mounted regiment. It was indispensable for shoeing or replacing horseshoes. Driving was done by the Wagon Trains which sent a complete team for each of the Guard's mounted regiments.

The furnace of the forge consisted of a sheet metal container and the heat from the embers was fed by a huge bellows at the rear.

Among the tools, there were the anvil and the bucket, and a casket containing all the blacksmith's tools and very likely spare horseshoes. The blacksmith however was a regimental master craftsman.

The field forge was normally drawn by a team of four horses, or on accessible terrain, by two horses. There was another lighter model with two wheels drawn by two horses.

The Medical Service

There were two elements in the Medical Service: the surgeon-majors, assistant-majors and under-assistant majors, incorporated into the various regiments of the Guard and mentioned on their rolls. In practice they wore the uniform with the Medical Service distinctives on their collars and facings.

The other element was the Gros-Caillou hospital which might have been situated towards the Rue Saint-Dominique in the 7th arrondissement of Paris. The institution was destroyed when the Rue Sedillot was driven through in 1896.

The Hospital

This hospital was originally built in 1759 by Maréchal de Biron for the French Guards and was especially assigned to the Guard; it was headed by a chief doctor, J. Sue; a Chief-Surgeon, J.D. Larrey; a Chief-Pharmacist Sureau, with clerks for administrating and supplying the hospital under the supervision of a War Commissioner.

When the Guard was campaigning, the chief-surgeon formed an ambulance, which today we would call a military field hospital with a group of surgeons and pharmacists and the transport needed for the hospital to work, including wagons for carrying the wounded, hospital wagons carrying equipment and the field forge.

The wagons were driven by a company of administration workers then later, the Guard's Wagon Train itself. The nursing service was carried out by a company of the Administration workers. We think that the military hospital nurses were dressed in grey as were the nurses created by Percy assigned to the Grande Armée.

The Guard had its own medical service headed by a Chief-Physician, Joseph Sue (father of the novelist Eugène Sue), a Chief Surgeon Dominique Larrey and a Chief Pharmacist Marie-Mathieu Surreau.

Joseph Sue was not disposed towards anything military, so much so that he couldn't even ride a horse – the excuse he gave for not following the army into Russia and returning to Paris, a fact which was never held against him since he was close to the Beauharnais family.

On the other hand, J.D. Larrey was everywhere, on all the battlefields, from the Egyptian Campaign to Waterloo. With Percy, he was the creator of emergency military medicine, setting up a system which went to the wounded; they were also at the origins of the mobile field ambulances which transported the wounded to the frontline hospitals and then ensured they were evacuated to the rear.

Better lot than the others

Once again, this organisation enabled the wounded in the Guard to have a better lot than the others. The management of the hospital was assisted by five surgeons and five first, second and third-class pharmacists.

In 1811, the hospital's strength was increased by twenty surgeons and five pharmacists, all classes included.

This strength grew again because, at the end of the Empire, there were two more doctors, 41 surgeons and 16 pharmacists. The nurses came from the 4th Company of the Administrative Workers' Battalion.

It was Napoleon who personally appointed the health officers put forward by the colonel-generals. These officers had no disciplinary powers over the soldiers and could not give health leave or authorise any absences. They were not part of the officer corps and as a result bore no rank markings except those specific to the Medical Service.

Organising the personnel and the materiel was supervised by a War Commissioner whose job was to look after the hospitals (12 August 1812 Regulations); the medical personnel had no say in the matter.

Administrating the hospital was the role of a hospital administration corps. Simply speaking the health officers were restricted to practising their art. The value of their work was rewarded by the Légion d'Honneur, or even titles in the empire's nobility for some of them.

When the Guard was campaigning, the hospital set up a field station made up of the personnel needed for it to function, the transport wagons, the mobile ambulances and their supply wagons. The Wagon Train of the Guard drove the teams after 1811.

As well as the hospital, each regiment of the Guard had a surgeon-major, an aide-major and an under aide-major on its staff.

The Uniform

The health service's dress was regulated by the decree dated 23 September 1803.

The background was cornflower blue with three distinctive colours: black for the doctors, scarlet or scarlet velvet for the surgeons, green velvet for the pharmacists.

The coat had no lapels and was buttoned straight down by nine buttons decorated with an eagle and the Epidaurus.

In full dress, the coat was decorated with nine buttonholes on the coat itself and two on the collar, three on the facings and the pockets for the first class.

For the undress uniform the coat had two buttonholes on the collar and three on the facings.

The second class had buttonholes on the collar, the facings and on the pocket only. The undress uniform had two buttonholes on the collar.

The third class had them on the collar and the facings and the undress uniform coat had one buttonhole on the collar.

The coat was worn with a gold aglet, at least in theory, since it does not appear on certain portraits of doctors in the Guard. The hat was identical in the whole health service, black with no stripes, with a gold cockade cord.

The jacket was the colour of the job. The breeches were cornflower blue or white depending on the season. The boots had turndowns or were *à l'écuyère*.

The 1812 text did not modify the hospital's health officer's uniform, which seems to contradict some of pictures where coats with lapels are being worn.

(suite page 146)

The Medical Service

Surgeon-major from the Grenadiers à pied of the Guard, according to a water colour by Knötel.

Surgeon-major in the Tirailleurs-Grenadiers à pied of the Guard, according to Plate N°40 by Rigo.

Surgeon-major from the 2nd Tirailleurs-Grenadiers of the Guard, according to a coat preserved in the Musée de l'Emperi.

Surgeon-major from the 4th Tirailleurs-Grenadiers of the Guard, according to a period miniature.

Surgeon-aide major from the Chasseurs à Cheval of the Guard in Paris.

Surgeon-major from the First Regiment d'Eclaireurs, or from the 1st Gardes d'Honneur, according to a miniature in the Musée de l'Empéri.

Surgeon-major from the Dragoons of the Guard, according to a coat preserved in the Musée de l'Armée à Paris.

Surgeon-aide-major from the Emperor's Household, according to a drawing by Rigo.

Larrey, at the beginning of its career, operates on the battlefield. *(Private collection, Rights Reserved)*

(continued from page 142)

J.D. Larrey was an exception and wore a uniform of his own.

The ambulance

This type of ambulance was created by J.D. Larrey, Chief-Surgeon of the Guard and Percy, Chief-Surgeon of the Grande Armée.

The idea was to bring the medical service as close as possible to the lines, and not the opposite and in order to do this, to design a wagon capable of carrying the wounded who could no longer walk or could barely be moved, in as much comfort as possible.

The chassis of the ambulance was entirely suspended and mounted on a platform designed in exactly the same way as the wagons. The four-wheel model was drawn by four horses with two drivers. It could carry four wounded.

Among the mobile ambulances, there was a contemporary drawing of a two-wheeled model drawn by two horses.

The carriage seems to have been suspended in the same way as the four-wheel ambulance. The description with the original drawings show that access was through the rear or from the front, but what was the point since there was no way in from the front.

Concerning the colour, we are not sure that the wagons were light ochre; however, we have used this colour since it appears on an engraving; it might however have been darker but we don't think they were made of plain varnished wood, which would have been too fragile for the weather conditions. Artillery green was not likely either since the idea was not for the wagons not to be confused with military materiel.

The field hospital wagon

Wagons followed the field hospitals, transporting all the supplies needed for wartime medical service.

The following is taken from a letter from Chirurgien-Aide-Major Thuriot, sent to Napoleon in 1805. Apart from denouncing the health service's organisation shortfalls, the bureaucratic and fastidious spirit shown by the war commissioners, the bad will of the suppliers when preparing the materiel needed for operating the field hospitals properly, the surgeon described the contents of a wagon: two mattresses, six strap stretchers, a cask of surgical instruments; 50 kilos of shredded linen, 100 kilos of bandages

and that there was only a single wagon per regiment of the Line, or more than a thousand men.

The description of the wagon gives an insight into the equipment available to the surgeons. How was the Guard in all this?

We have no exact references about the organisation.

We simply think that it must have been better organised and as a result, must have had better equipment and more of it.

Chief doctor in wearing campaign dress.

Chief doctor wearing undress uniform after a coat preserved in the Musée de l'Emperi.

Chief-Surgeon wearing campaign dress.

Coat preserved in the Delft (Holland) Military Museum, which belonged to a surgeon, third class, who had taken part in the Russian Campaign.

Surgeon, Second Class, wearing campaign dress.

Doctor, First Class, wearing full dress, according to Commandant Bucquoy's set of cards.

Surgeon, Second Class, wearing undress uniform after Weiland.

Clerk from the Hospital Administration of the Guard at what was called the Gros Caillou, located in Paris in the quarter of the same name.

The Medical Service

Under the tent, the baron Larrey – chief surgeon of the Imperial Guard – in a mobile field hospital in 1813, during the Prussian Campaign. *(Engraving by Jack Girbal, for plates by Dr Hourtoulle, Private collection, RR)*

SECOURS AUX BRAVES

The ambulance

Dominique Larrey and Pierre François Percy were the inventors of emergency medical care. In 1792, Larrey conceived a mobile field hospital capable getting close to the battlefield and as near as possible to the wounded.

The idea was to bring the medical service as close as possible to the lines, and not the opposite and in order to do this, to design a wagon capable of carrying the wounded who could no longer walk or could barely be moved, in as much comfort as possible. The chassis of the ambulance was entirely suspended and mounted on a platform designed in exactly the same way as the wagons. The four-wheel model was drawn by four horses with two drivers. It could carry four wounded.

The light Ambulance

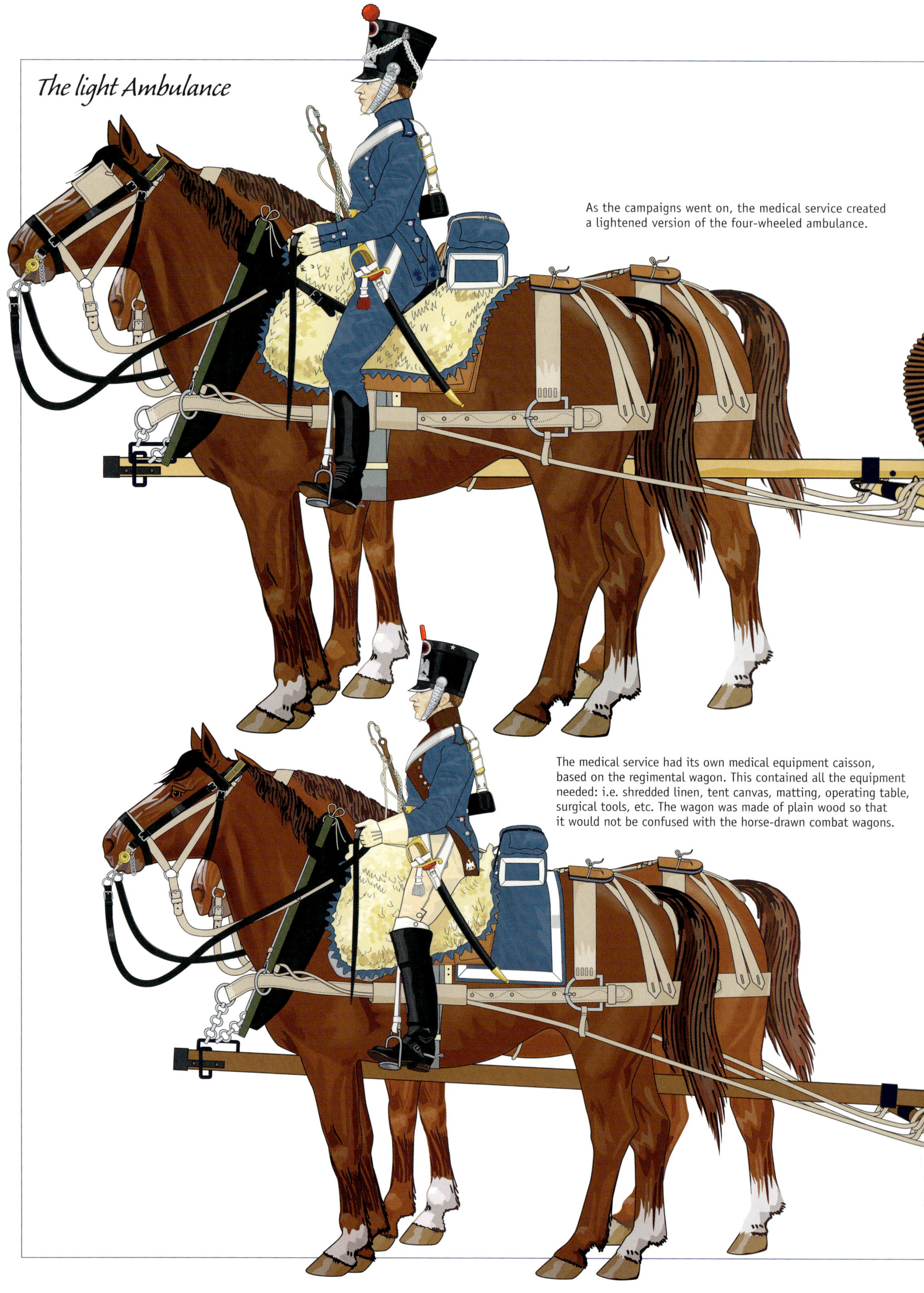

As the campaigns went on, the medical service created a lightened version of the four-wheeled ambulance.

The medical service had its own medical equipment caisson, based on the regimental wagon. This contained all the equipment needed: i.e. shredded linen, tent canvas, matting, operating table, surgical tools, etc. The wagon was made of plain wood so that it would not be confused with the horse-drawn combat wagons.

AMBULANCE
GARDE IMPÉRIALE
GARDE IMPÉRIALE
AMBULANCE.

The Great headquarters

As was mentioned at the beginning of the chapter, the Guard comprised four large corps to which was attached headquarters staff.

Marshalls and Generals

The Maréchal de France who had the title of Colonel-General had a chief-of-staff with the rank of Brigadier or Major-General and a variable number of aide de camps.

In theory, the aide de camp attached to the Guard wore the regulation uniform with the aglet and button with an eagle of the Guard. Like all the corps in the Grande Armée, the headquarters staff included an adjudant-commandant who was a colonel; he could be a major-general in the Guard, assisted by other officers. There was most certainly an ingénieur-cartographe (map-maker) among these officers and here again the uniform was the same as all his engineer colleagues except for the button with an eagle. On the general staff, the "intelligent" arm was represented by a senior officer from the Artillery and the Engineers. At the beginning of the Empire, these officers were detached from a corps of the Line before the creation of the Foot Artillery and the Engineers of the Guard.

The ordnance officers

The ordnance officers were not part of the Guard Staff Corps, but they were there to transmit orders received directly from Napoleon. Although they were mainly junior officers, they were the direct representatives of the Emperor with any divisional or corps commander who had to obey any order brought by an ordnance officer.

There twelve of them and they were in the Guard until 1809. in order to limit the numbers on the Staff, they were later attached to the Emperor's Household. This was the opportunity for these officers to change uniform from green with gold embroidery to sky blue with silver embroidery.

In his organisation decree dated 29 July 1804, the Guard comprised four big commands:

A colonel-general commanding the Grenadiers à pied, Maréchal Davout.

A colonel-general commanding the Chasseurs à pied, Maréchal Soult.

A colonel-general commanding the Artillery and the Sailors, Maréchal Mortier.

A colonel-general commanding the Cavalry of the Guard, Maréchal Bessières replaced on 18 November 1812 by Maréchal Suchet.

The adjudant-commandant

The adjudant-commandants and their officiers-adjoints were allotted to each colonel-general, 12 aide de camps, a battalion commander in the Engineers and a captain from the Engineers attached to the Grande Armée, because the Engineers battalion did not exist at that time.

To this must be added the ingénieurs-géographes, among whom the best-known was Barcler d'Albe who was in Napoleon's direct service.

The colonel-generals received their orders directly from Napoleon for everything concerning the service of the Guard.

When the second organisation took place in 1806, the colonel-generals were unchanged; there were the same general staff, four aide de camps with the rank of colonel, 20 aide de camps from the rank of squadron commander to lieutenant, a battalion commander from the Engineers and two captains, an assistant and a librarian.

In 1809, Napoleon decided to reduce the hierarchy of the Guard's general staff in Spain and the Emperor's general-aide de camps were no longer part of the Guard.

Likewise, the aide de camps of the colonel-generals and the generals who had the functions of a colonel commanding a regiment of the Guard (do not forget that a colonel-major in the Guard was a major-general or brigadier-general) were no longer on the strength of the Guard.

The principle of the rank in the Guard being equivalent to the rank immediately above it in the Grande Armée applied to these men. Basically, after a length of service in the Guard, the aide de camps or the personnel on the headquarters staff were appointed to command posts higher up in the Cavalry or the Infantry.

The dress of the headquarters staff, i.e. the adjudant-commandants, the officiers-adjoints, respected the 1803 Regulations. To distinguish themselves from the Grande Armée, they wore a gold aglet corresponding to the metal of the button, and the buttons were stamped with an eagle of the Guard.

The aide de camps, known as a general rule for their rather fanciful dress usually due to their private means, were not over-zealous dress-wise when in the immediate vicinity of Napoleon and respected the 1803 Regulations, i.e. a dark blue coat with sky blue distinctives and eagle-stamped buttons.

On 19 September 1806, by decree, Napoleon created ordnance officers for sending his orders quickly. They were placed under the command of Caulaincourt, the grand-equerry, and were counted among the Cavalry of the Guard. Article 1 of the decree stated that there were twelve officers from captain down to sous-lieutenant.

They ensured there was someone on permanent duty with the Emperor, and when he was campaigning, followed him every time he went out. Each officer had to have four horses he could ride and four following him, with as many servants and grooms. So as to be able to pay for equipment and maintenance expenses, each officer had to receive a revenue of 6000 francs from his family, which shows that there was a selection process and that most of the officers came from the old nobility and the large wealthy families of the Empire. They also received a further 6000 francs from Napoleon as their pay of a first captain of cavalry of the Guard.

Like the aide de camps, the ordnance officers were withdrawn from the Guard to be attached directly to the Emperor's household.

Aides de camps

The aides de camps were junior officers on the staff trusted with transmitting orders from the general to whom they were assigned. This was no sinecure: they had to be able to understand and transcribe, in spi-

(continued on page 158)

The coat of arms
of Maréchal Bessières.

The Maréchal Bessières

Bessières started his military career in the Constitutional Guard under Louis XVI in 1791. In 1793, he joined the Army of the Pyrenées and obtained his lieutenant's and captain's stripes.
He joined the 22nd Chasseurs in the Army of Italy. On 14 January 1797, he distinguished himself at the Battle of Rivoli where he was promoted to Major. On 9 March 1799, he was promoted to the rank of brigade commander. During the Expedition to Egypt, he was promoted to commander of the Corps des Guides by Napoleon.
Having taken part in the *coup d'état* of 18 Brumaire, as a reward, he was appointed second-in-command of the Consular Guard. On 14 June 1800 at Marengo, he was made a brigadier-general; on 13 September 1802 he was made a major-general. In 1804 he was on the list of *maréchaux*.
In 1805, Bessières commanded the Guard. In Poland, he led the newly-formed cavalry reserve. In 1808, Bessières was sent to Spain to head an army corps. In 1809, Bessières was made Duke of Istria and once again the commanding officer of the Cavalry of the Guard. In 1811, he was Governor in Spain.
In 1812, he was at the head of the Guard, for the Russian Campaign. For the Saxon Campaign in 1813, he was given the command of all the cavalry.
He was killed by a cannonball on 1 May 1813 at Weissenfels.

Bessières wearing
his favourite *à la chasseur*
tailcoat.

Marshals
Regulation full dress.
Regulation 1798 undress uniform.
Epaulette and mark
of Maréchal de France.
Regulation full dress.
Uniform in frock coat.

Generals officers

Major-general in the Guard on campaign in 1809, after the Martinet Collection.

General officer, aide de camp to the Emperor wearing full dress.

General aide de camp wearing campaign dress.

General Rottembourg's uniform he was a major-general in the Guard during the 1814 Campaign for France, after a painting by Phillipoteaux preserved in the Musée de l'Armée de Paris.

The adjudants-commandants

Adjudant-commandant wearing full dress at the end of the Consular period, according to a drawing by P. Benigni in Commandant Bucquoy's set of cards.

Adjudant-commandant wearing a frock coat.

Adjudant-commandant wearing undress uniform.

Braid, button and turnbacks decoration for an officer adjoint.

Officer adjoint wearing full dress, according to Rigo.

Officer adjoint wearing campaign dress, according to P. Courcelle.

The adjudants-commandant

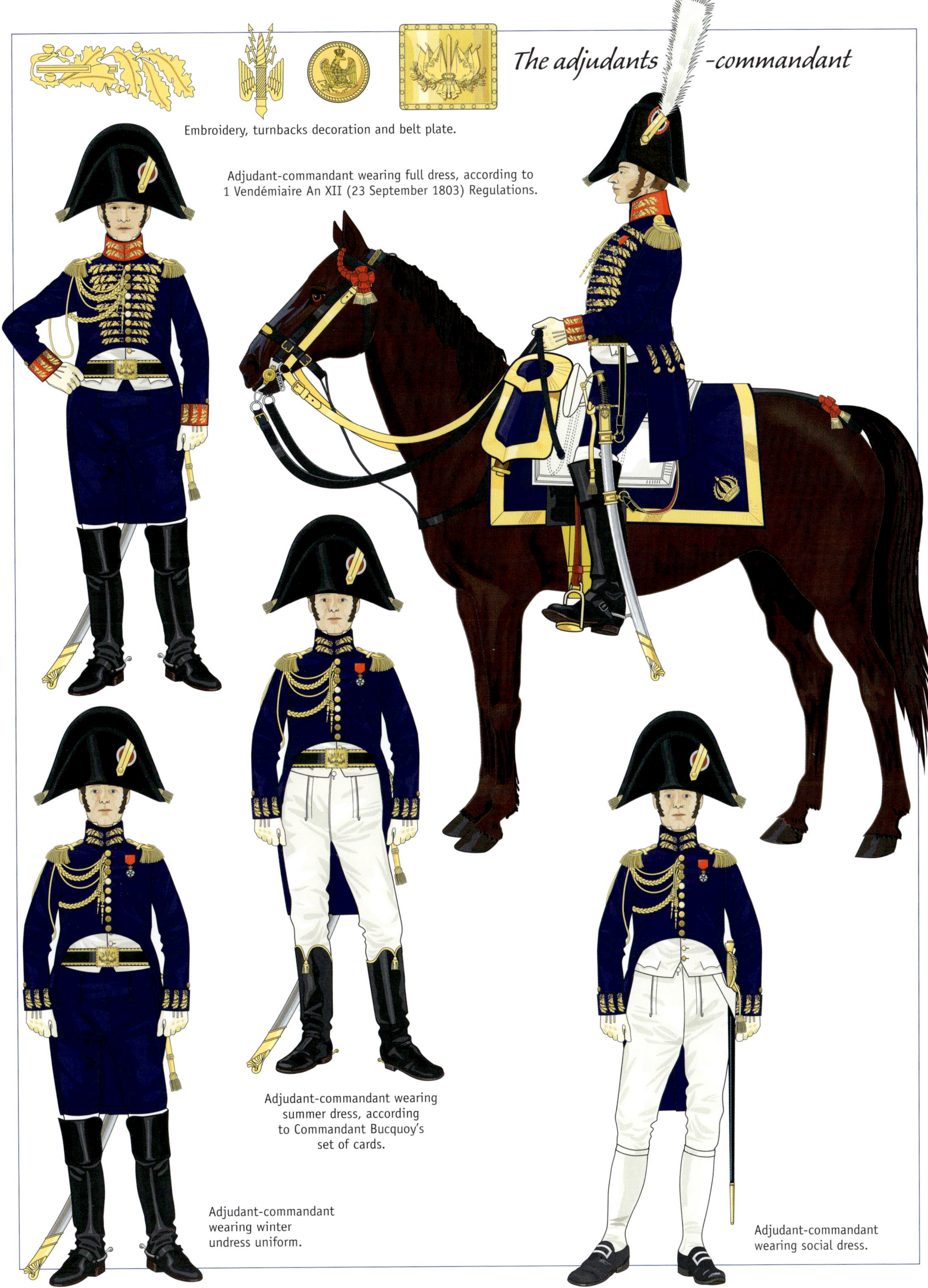

Embroidery, turnbacks decoration and belt plate.

Adjudant-commandant wearing full dress, according to 1 Vendémiaire An XII (23 September 1803) Regulations.

Adjudant-commandant wearing summer dress, according to Commandant Bucquoy's set of cards.

Adjudant-commandant wearing winter undress uniform.

Adjudant-commandant wearing social dress.

The maréchal Bessières, at the head of the Cavalry and the complete Headquarter of the Guard in Berlin. *(Engraving by Victor Huen, Private collection, Rights reserved)*

(continued from page 152)
rit, the orders they were given, if not in certain circumstances to carry them out themselves, to pass through the lines without getting caught knowing that the enemy was always keen to get hold of information about what was happening on, the other side, to know about troop movements and to understand what was happening on, the battlefield and finally in return to give oral reports from corps commanders.

Note that the function paid a heavy tribute in Spain where the lines of communication were particularly unsure.

The *ingénieurs géographes*

Map-making at the time was still rather basic, but the military needed more accurate mapping for the troop movements. The *Ingénieur-Géographe* (Engineer-cartographer or map-maker) was capable of taking topological readings of the terrain where the battle was going to take place, drawing a scale map with its contour lines, making panoramic drawings of the countryside which faced the armies.

To do this he had measuring and drawing instruments together with a mapping table.

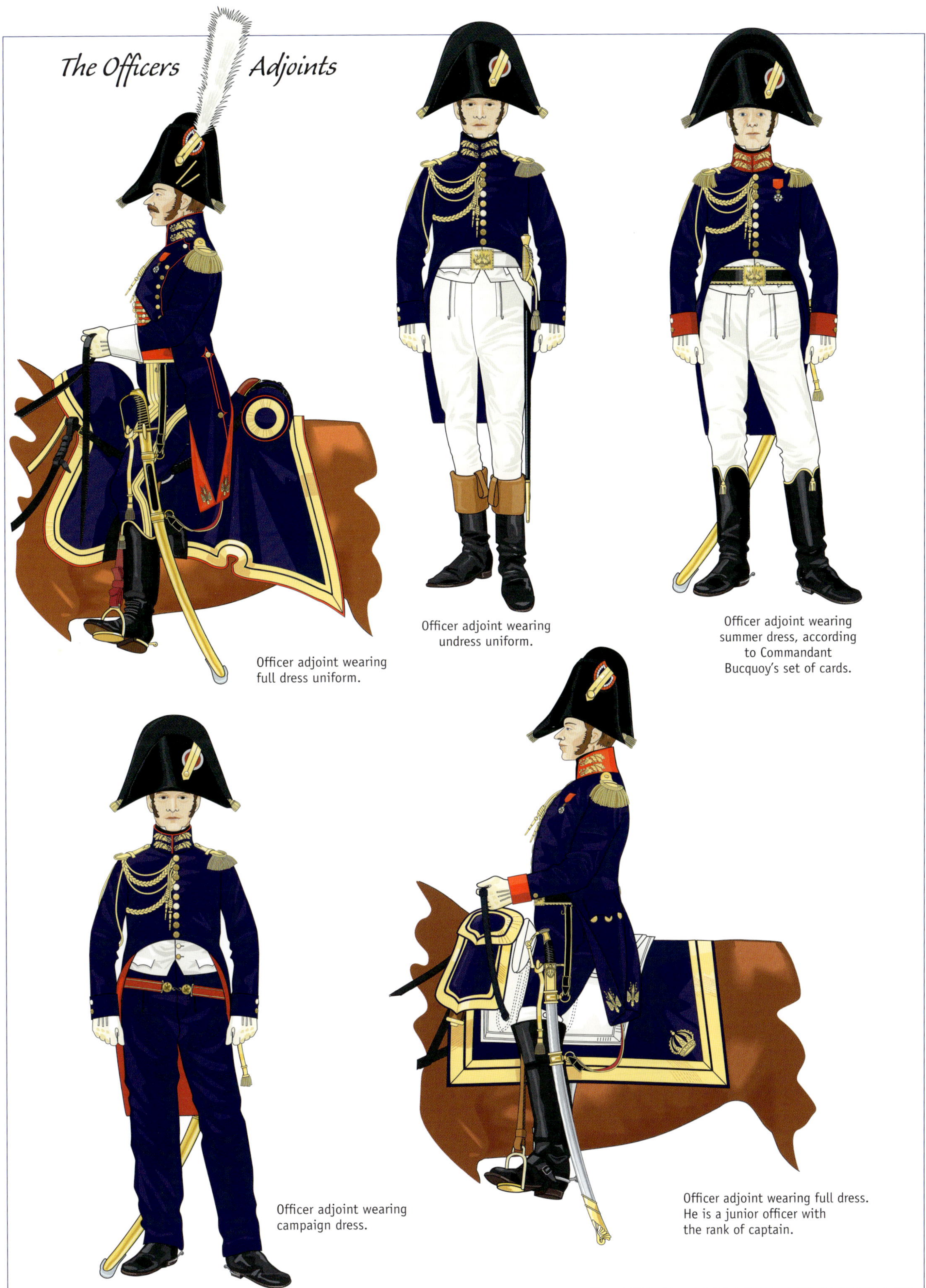

Officer adjoint wearing full dress uniform.

Officer adjoint wearing undress uniform.

Officer adjoint wearing summer dress, according to Commandant Bucquoy's set of cards.

Officer adjoint wearing campaign dress.

Officer adjoint wearing full dress. He is a junior officer with the rank of captain.

The attached Officers

Engineer captain attached to headquarters wearing full dress.

Engineer captain attached to headquarters wearing an overcoat.

Senior Engineers officer from the Guard attached to headquarters, before 1808.

Senior Artillery officer from the Guard attached to headquarters, before 1810.

Junior Artillery officer from the Guard attached to headquarters.

The ingénieurs-géographes

Senior *ingénieur-géographe* officer wearing full dress, after Malibran.

Engineer Captain wearing campaign dress, according to the 1812 Regulations.

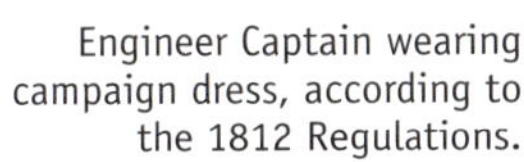

Engineer Captain wearing campaign dress, according to the 1812 Regulations.

Belt plate, according to an example preserved in the Musée de l'Armée in Paris.

Belt plate, according to the 1812 Regulations.

Engineer Captain wearing a frock coat, according to the 1812 Regulations.

The aides de camp

Aide de camp wearing *à la hussarde* dress. He is not wearing an aglet since theoretically it was not worn on the dolman.

Aide de camp to Maréchal Bessières.

Aide de camp to Maréchal Bessières, rear view.

Aide de camp attached to a division of the Guard.

Aide de camp attached to a division of the Guard.

The aides de camp

Aide de camp attached to a division of the Guard, after notes taken by Surgeon-Major Lévêque.

Aide de camp attached to a division of the Guard.

Aide de camp attached to a division of the Guard wearing-tailcoat

Aide de camp.

Aide de camp attached to a division of the Guard wearing an overcoat.

Aide de camp attached to a division of the Guard wearing campaign dress, according to a drawing by L. Rousselot.

The aides de camp

Aide de camp wearing regualtion sack coat.

Aide de camp to a major-general in 1812, after a water colour by Knötel.

Aide de camp, according to the book by L. Fallou devoted to the Guard.

Aide de camp in sack coat.

Aide de camp wearing regulation Hussar uniform.

The Emperor's eyeglass page. This page belonged to the Emperor's Household and is wearing the Imperial Household's specific green coat.

Shoulder strap.

Rear view.

Horse equipment: saddlecloth made of cloth edged with gold braid and Hungarian-style harnessing.

The Ordnance officers

Ordnance officer wearing full dress 1806-1807, after a drawing by P. Courcelle and Rigo, showing him on foot.

Ordnance officer wearing undress uniform 1806-1807, after a drawing by E. Lelièpvre.

Ordnance officer wearing an overcoat.

Ordnance officer wearing full dress 1806-1807, according to la Garde by L. Fallou.

Ordnance officer wearing marching dress, according to P. Courcelle.

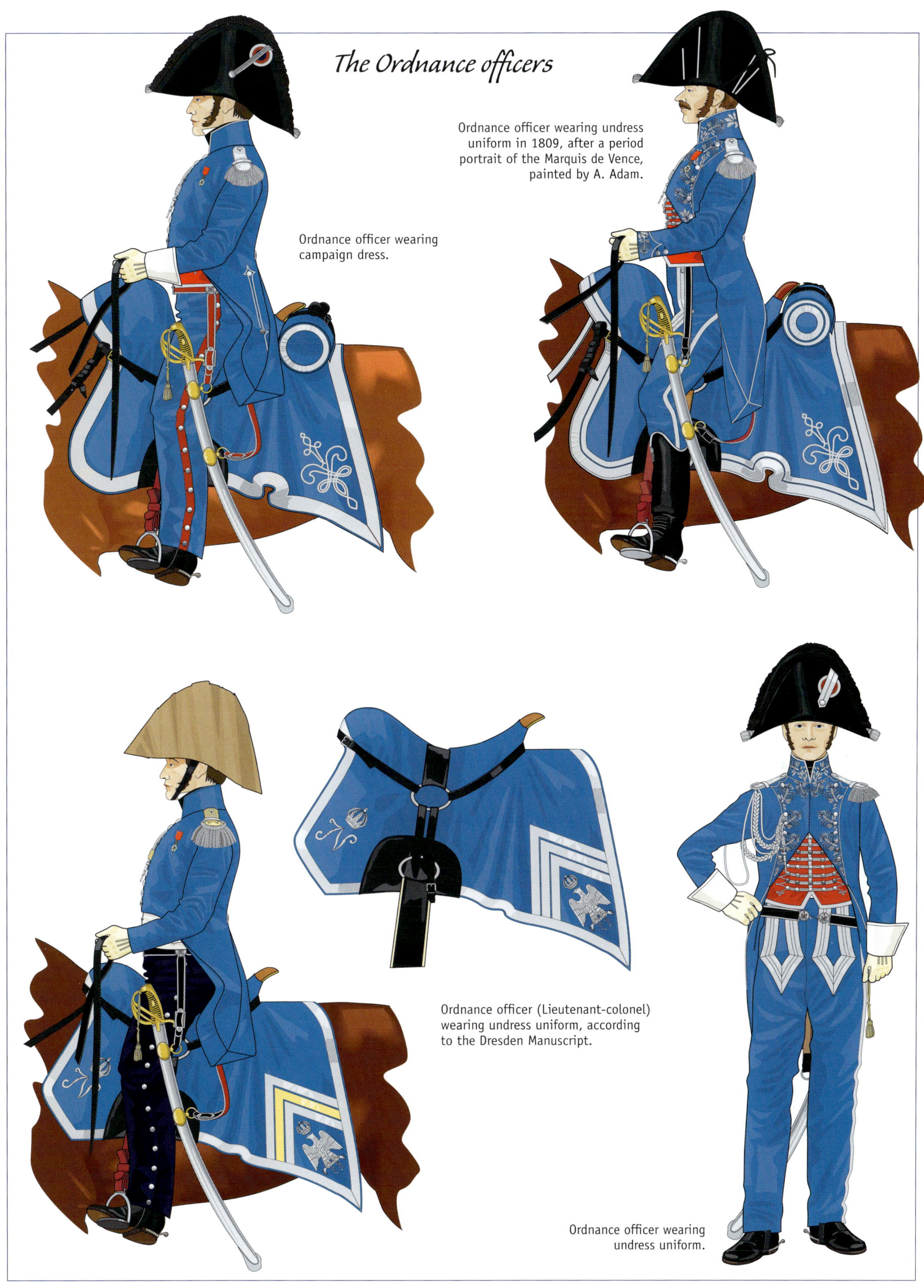

The Ordnance officers

Ordnance officer wearing campaign dress.

Ordnance officer wearing undress uniform in 1809, after a period portrait of the Marquis de Vence, painted by A. Adam.

Ordnance officer (Lieutenant-colonel) wearing undress uniform, according to the Dresden Manuscript.

Ordnance officer wearing undress uniform.

The Ordnance officers
Ordnance officer wearing full dress in 1809, after a period portrait of the Marquis de Montesquiou, painted by A. Adam.
Ordnance officer wearing full dress in 1809, after a period portrait of the Marquis de Vence, painted by A. Adam.
Aglet.
Rank epaulette and counter epaulette.
Horse equipment.
Ordnance officer wearing full dress in 1809-1811.

Constant, the Emperor's Valet

Constant, the Emperor's valet wearing marching dress.

Constant
in full dress uniform.

Constant Wairy was born in Péruwelz (Belgium) in 1178. He entered Joséphine Bonaparte's service on 21 April 1799. He accompanied the Emperor on his campaigns from 1805 to 1813. After the fall of the Empire, he went back to Belgium then to France in the Eure department. He died on 27 June 1845.

The Emperor's valet
on campaign.

Appendix - The Administration of the Imperial Guard

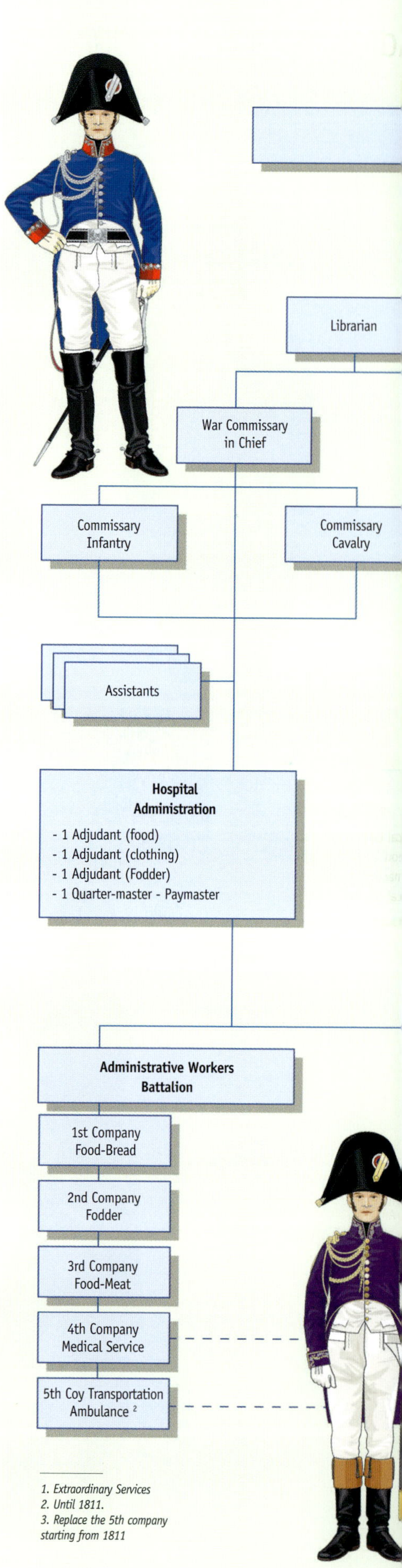

The Guard had its own administration organised like the Grande Armée's. it was divided into two main corps: the War Commissioners whose job it was to supervise the Supply Corps and the Guard's hospital. The Parade Inspectors were responsible for the organisation, the integration and running of the men as well as the pay and accounting in each corps. Every year, the Guard was reviewed by the Inspector Generals who reported on the strength and the movement of personnel, clothing, equipment and weapons in order to find out what was going to be needed for the following year. Lower down, the under-inspectors reviewed each regiment quarterly.

Guillaume Peyrusse, the Paymaster-General, received the funds from the Imperial Treasury to pay personnel and for war equipment. He was assisted by the Payer-Generals, Assistant-Payers and secretaries whose job it was to keep a tally of the movement of funds and to supply the receipts needed for the expenses. We know from an article published in an SCFH bulletin, how a paymaster-general dressed and we have presumed that for the Guard, he wore the aglet the same colour as his gold buttons stamped with an eagle.

The Administration workers

The Administration workers were organised according to the decree dated 1 May 1806. There were five companies, each comprising 5 sergeants, 12 corporals, 52 bakers, 15 butchers, 15 foragers, 42 soldiers for the ambulance wagons, a trumpeter and a blacksmith. These Administrative Workers were reorganised several times as the Guard grew progressively larger. From five companies they grew to battalion strength. From five companies they grew to battalion strength under the command of a war commissioner. In 1811, their number increased in preparation for the invasion of Russia and from the return of this campaign up to the First Abdication, the companies were made up by conscripts and volunteers.

According to Commandant Bucquoy's card collection, the coat worn at the beginning of the Empire was tailored in the same way as for the Infantry, but it was sky blue with white lapels. We also know of the mounted worker's uniform: short coats with square lapels, cut in the same way as the Cuirassiers, sky-blue or iron grey. The difference between these two colours is barely perceptible on the documents. Note that L. Fallou, in his history of the Imperial Guard, mentions an iron grey background on a coat, and that Marco de Saint-Hilaire, in his own work on the Imperial Guard, also describes it, stating that it was a short iron grey coat with pointed lapels like the Artillery Train's. Finally, thanks to H. Boissellier and Commandant Bucquoy, we know what the uniforms at the end of the Empire looked like, like the *habit-veste* cut according to the 1812 Regulations.

dministration of the Imperial Guard

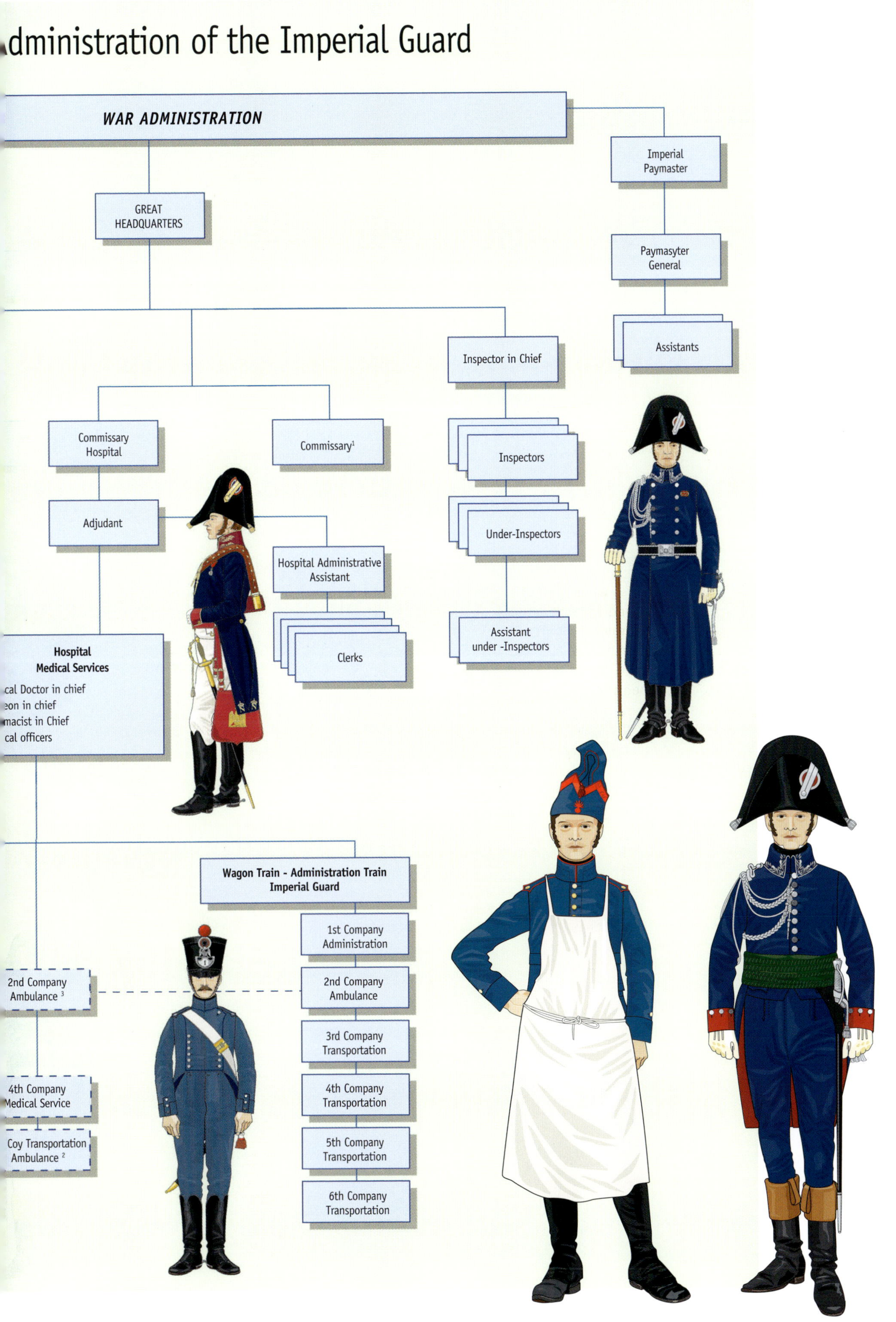

Sources and Bibliography

PRIMARY SOURCES

I. Archives from SHD
Xab 4. La Garde consulaire à pied et à cheval; *Xab 10*. La Vieille Garde; *Xab 12*.

II. French National Archives
« Bulletin des lois de la République »

« AF IV 540*. Garde consulaire; *AF IV* 80; AFIV*187; AF IV* 1 705-1 706*. Garde impériale ».

III. Library from musée de l'Armée
« Collections des décrets ».

Bibliothèque Nationale, cabinet des estampes.
« Recueil de Valmont ».

MEMOIRS

« La vie militaire sous le Premier Empire », Elzéar Blaze, collection « Mémoire d'Empire », Éditions Jacob Duvernet, 2011, Paris.

BOOKS

« Napoléon's Soldiers », le manuscrit de Otto, compilé par G. Dempsey, Arms and Armour Press.

« Les Uniformes du Premier Empire », suites de costumes publiées par Martinet, compilées par Bertrand Malvaux, Éditions du Canonnier, Nantes, 2008.

« Dictionnaires des armées de Terre et de mer - Encyclopédie militaire et maritime », comte de Chesnel, Armand le Chevallier éditeur, Paris, 1864.

« Dictionnaire biographique des généraux et amiraux français de la Révolution et de l'Empire », Georges Six, Georges Saffroy Éditeur, Paris, 1934.

« Guide à l'usage des artistes et des costumiers », H. Malibran, Verlag, Heere der vergangenheit, J. Olmes Kreffeld, 1972.

« Les uniformes de l'Armée française depuis 1690 à nos jours », Lienhart et Humbert, Paris.

« La Grande Armée », Victor Huen, Herscher, 2004.

« L'armée de Napoléon, organisation et vie quotidienne », Alain Pigeard, Tallandier, 2000.

« Dictionnaire de la Grande Armée », Alain Pigeard, Bibliothèque napoléonienne, Talllandier, Paris, 2002.

« Napoleonic Wars, Napoleon's Army », R. Chartrand, Brassey.

« Les Uniformes du Premier Empire, La cavalerie de la Garde impériale », Commandant Bucquoy, Paris, Jacques Grancher éditeur.

« Les boutons français », L. Fallou. Éditions du Canonnier.

« Uniformes du Premier Empire », F.-G. Hourtoulle, J. Girbal. Histoire & Collections, 2007.

« Napoleonic Uniforms », colonel J. R. Elting, Emperor Press.

« Les uniformes et les armes des soldats du Premier Empire » tome II, Liliane & Fred Funcken. Casterman, 1968.

« Drapeaux et étendards du Premier Empire », Pierre Charrié, Rigo. Copernic.

« Aigles et shakos du Premier Empire », Christian Blondiau, Armes & Uniformes, 1979.

« Uniformes des armées de Waterloo », U. Pericoli. Éditions Vila.

« Les armées de Waterloo », Bernard Coppens. Éditions de la Belle Alliance, 1986.

« Armes à feu réglementaires » volumes I et II, Jean Boudriot, chez l'auteur, Paris.

« Armes blanches », les Cahiers de Christian Aries et Michel Pétard, chez l'auteur.

« Équipements militaires, 1600-1870 », tomes II, III IV et V. Michel Pétard, chez l'auteur, 1985, 1986, 1987, 1988.

« Histoire populaire de la Garde impériale », Marco de Saint-Hilaire, Paris, 1854.

« La Garde impériale », Louis Fallou, Paris, la Giberne, 1901.

« Napoléon et la Garde », Commandant Lachouque, Éditions Lavauzelle, Limoges, 1982.

« La Garde impériale, les troupes à cheval, volume III et volume IV », André Jouineau et Jean-Marie Mongin, Histoire & Collections, Paris, 2002.

« La Guardia Imperiale napoleonica. I reggimenti della vechia e Media Guardia », Vittorio Nino Novarese, Ermanno Albertelli Editore, Parma, 1996.

« Napoléon et la Russie, 1805-1807 », Jean Tranié et Juan-Carlos Carmignani, Copernic.

« Napoléon et l'Italie, 1805-1815 », Gilles Boué et Juan-Carlos Carmignani, Histoire & Collections, 2016.

« La cavalerie au temps des chevaux », Colonel Marcel Dugué Mac Carthy, EPA, 1989.

« La cavalerie française et son harnachement », Colonel Marcel Dugué Mac Carthy, Maloine, 1985.

Tomes I et IV des recueils du « *Règlement sur l'habit* » de Bardin.

MAGAZINES

« Les Gardes d'honneur », Christian Blondiau, Uniformes n° 47.

« Le gendarme d'élite », Michel Pétard, Uniformes.

« L'artilleur à cheval de la Garde impériale » Uniformes.

UNIFORM PLATES

« Les uniformes de l'armée française », Lucien Rousselot, Paris
Plate n° 95. « gendarmerie d'élite de la Garde, 1801-1815 »
Plate n° 60. « L'artillerie à cheval de la Garde impériale, I »
Plate n° 74. « L'artillerie à cheval de la Garde impériale, II »
Plate n° 45. « Grenadiers à cheval de la Garde, trompettes, 1804-1815
Plate n° 100. « Train d'artillerie de la Garde, 1800-1815 ».
Plate n° 106. « Train d'artillerie de la Garde, 1800-1815 ».

Plates « Le plumet », Albert Rigondeau dit Rigo
Plate n° 6. « Gendarmerie d'Élite, timbalier, 1806 ».
Plate n° 13. « Guidon de l'artillerie à cheval de la Garde, 1813 ».
Plate n° 18. « Jean-Baptiste Bessières, colonel-général de la cavalerie ».
Plate n° 43. « Officier d'ordonnance de Napoléon 1er ».
Plate n° 50. « Colonel-major du 4e régiment de Gardes d'Honneur ».
Plate n° 57. « Colonelde la gendarmerie d'élite, 1806 ».
Plate n° 85. « Aide de camp du maréchal Berthier ».
Plate n° 100. « Larrey en Uniforme de chirurgien en chef de la Grande Armée, 1812 ».
Plate n° 105. « Les tartares lithuaniens, 1813-1814 ».
Plate n° 113. « Jean-Jacques Desvaux de Saint Maurice, commandant en chef de l'artilleriede la Garde, 1815 ».
Plate n° 115. « Étendard de l'artillerie à cheval de la Garde, 1815 ».
Plate n° 118. « Officier adjoint de l'état-major de la Garde ».
Plate n° 176. « Gendarmes d'ordonnance, Trompette, 1809 ».
Plate n° 228. « Chef d'escadron en grande tenue des Tartares lithuaniens, 1813 ».

Lithuanians Tartars, in 1813, and the diversity of their uniforms, drawing by Eugène Lelièpvre. *(RR, private collection)*

Contents

Next page.
Officer from the Regiment of Grenadiers à cheval of the Imperial Guard wearing full dress.
(Drawing by Eugène Lelièpvre, RR, private collection)

Thanks

We would like to thank and pay tribute here to Rigo "le Plumet", Michel Pétard, Dr François-Guy Hourtoulle, Juan-Carlos Carmignani, Bernard Giovanangeli and Jean-Louis Viau.
Their example, their work, their precious help – as much morale-wise as editorial – has been with us all the time, ever since we started this big project in 1998.
Once again we pay tribute to all of our illustrious predecessors.
Thanks also to Georges Bernage, a brave publisher, for allowing us to realise this project.

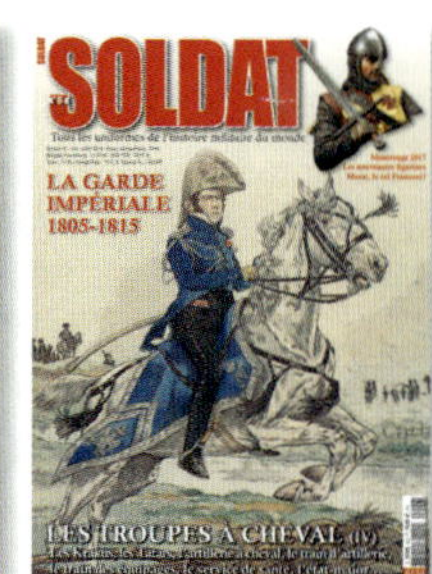

Already been published in the form of the fifth and sixth numbers of the magazine *"SOLDAT – les uniformes de l'histoire militaire du Monde"* in March and May 2018 for Editions Heimdal.

André Jouineau drew the 130 uniform plates in this book.
André Jouineau and Jean-Marie Mongin wrote the captions. The text is by Jean-Marie Mongin.
The drawings and organograms were realised by Jean-Marie Mongin with the help of André Jouineau.
Conception, mock-up and layout by André Jouineau and Jean-Marie Mongin.
Cover by Jean-Marie Mongin for Editions Heimdal.
The translation was by Alan Mckay

Éditions Heimdal BP 61,350 - 14,406 Bayeux CEDEX
Téléphone: 02 31 51 68 68 - Fax: 02 3,151 68 60.
www.editions-heimdal.fr

ISBN 978-84048-512-4

Print by Pollina (France),
May 2018 for *Editions Heimdal*
Georges Bernage, Editor.